THE SHELLEY LIBRARY

An Essay in Bibliography

BY

H. BUXTON FORMAN

I

SHELLEY'S OWN BOOKS PAMPHLETS & BROADSIDES
POSTHUMOUS SEPARATE ISSUES AND
POSTHUMOUS BOOKS WHOLLY
OR MAINLY BY
HIM

HASKELL HOUSE PUBLISHERS Ltd.
Publishers of Scarce Scholarly Books
NEW YORK. N. Y. 10012
1971

First Published 1886

HASKELL HOUSE PUBLISHERS Lᴛᴅ.
Publishers of Scarce Scholarly Books
280 LAFAYETTE STREET
NEW YORK, N. Y. 10012

Library of Congress Catalog Card Number: 78-116794

Standard Book Number 8383-1036-2

Printed in the United States of America

THE SHELLEY LIBRARY.

I.

HIS OWN BOOKS, PAMPHLETS, AND BROADSIDES; POSTHUMOUS SEPARATE ISSUES; AND POSTHUMOUS BOOKS WHOLLY OR MAINLY BY SHELLEY.

THE first division of this work deals with the *editiones principes* and with all separate reproductions of them. A collection of the first editions of Shelley's Works is not by any means a complete collection of all he left, because a large number of his compositions, both verse and prose, first appeared in newspapers, magazines, Lives, miscellaneous books, or collected editions. These will be described hereafter in several groups.

A first look at the present group will surprise many readers, who, though perhaps acquainted with the mass of Shelley's writings, were not aware how many separate appearances he made. It is not unlikely that many things remain to be discovered, such as the private issues of juvenile compositions mentioned in " A Newspaper Editor's Reminiscences," in *Fraser's Magazine* for June 1841. This hitherto unidentified worthy says at page 702 of the magazine in question, when speaking of Sir Bysshe Shelley, " It was his purse which supplied young Bysshe with the means of printing many of his fugitive pieces. These issued from the press of a printer at Horsham . . .; and although they were not got up in good style, the expense was much greater than Shelley could have afforded, if he had not received assistance from his grandfather." It may be doubted whether anything of great intrinsic merit or interest is any longer missing; but one may own without shame a curiosity to behold anything and everything that ever issued from the hand of the poet whose after achievements made his life and himself of the deepest interest. Gladly would I describe here any of those trifles which are thought to have issued from the press at Horsham; but for the present there is no help for our beginning to trace Shelley's tangible doings from the first half of the year 1810, when he was in his eighteenth year and put forth that veritable curiosity *Zastrozzi*.

ZASTROZZI.

Zastrozzi, which appears to be the first substantive work issued by Shelley, is a duodecimo volume, consisting of fly-title, *Zastrozzi,/ a Romance*, with imprint at foot, *Printed by S. Hamilton, Weybridge*, title-page as given below, and 252 pages of text with the head-line *Zastrozzi* throughout.

(1)

ZASTROZZI,

A ROMANCE.

BY

P. B. S.

——That their God
May prove their foe, and with repenting hand
Abolish his own works—This would surpass
Common revenge.

PARADISE LOST.

LONDON:
PRINTED FOR G. WILKIE AND J. ROBINSON,
57, PATERNOSTER ROW.

1810.

Generally when copies are found they are from circulating libraries, dirty and dilapidated; but they appear to have been issued in blue boards backed with drab, bearing the label "ZASTROZZI./A ROMANCE./ *Price 5s.*"

Medwin (*Shelley Papers*, 1833, page 10) says Shelley told him that some chapters of it were written by Harriet Grove, the poet's cousin and first love. Mr. D. F. MacCarthy (*Shelley's Early Life*, 1872, pages 11 and 12) records that it was published on the 5th of June 1810, and advertized in *The Times* on the 5th and 12th.

There are at least three extant letters of Shelley's (two of them
hitherto unpublished) bearing on the date of *Zastrozzi's* composition and publication. In one dated the 7th of May 1809
(Prose Works, Volume III, page 329), he says he means to finish
and publish "a Romance," of which he has already written "a
large portion," but does not expect "any pecuniary advantage."

The next letter, which is among the Montagu Letters in the
Bodleian Library, is addressed to Edward Graham, Esq., No.
29 Vine Street, Piccadilly, and is as follows :—

Eton, April 1, 1810

My dear Graham—

I will see you at Easter,—next Friday I shall be in
London, but for a very short time—unable to call on you till
Passion week—Robinson will take no trouble about the
reviewers, let every thing proper be done about the venal
villains and I will settle with you when we meet at Easter.—
We will all go in a posse to the bookseller's in Mr. Grove's
barouche & four—Shew them that we are no Grub Street
garretteers—but why Harriet more than any one else—a faint
essay I see in return for my enquiry for Caroline—

We will not be cheated again—let us come over Jock,[1] for if
he will not give me a devil of a price for my Poem & at
least £60 for my new Romance in three Volumes[2] the dog
shall not have them.

Pouch the reviewers—10£ will be sufficient I should suppose,
and that I can with the greatest ease repay when we meet at
Passion week. Send the reviews in which Zastrozzi is mentioned
to Field Place, the British review is the hardest, let that be
pouched well—My note of hand if for any larger sum is quite
at your service, as it is of consequence in fiction to establish
your name as high as you can in the literary lists—

Adieu
Yours most devotedly
Percy Bysshe Shelley

Let me hear how you proceed in the business of Reviewing.

P. B. S.

This curious letter, wildly practical for a boy of seventeen,
seems to indicate that the book was on the eve of publication—
perhaps just published. In the third letter, dated the 29th of

---

[1] J. Robinson, the publisher, I presume.

[2] Probably *St. Irvyne*: Shelley expressed surprise when Stockdale told him
it would only make one volume.

May 1810, also from Eton, and to the same correspondent,—a most interesting letter sold by Messrs. Sotheby & Co. on the 18th of January 1877 and not yet, I believe, published,—there is a postscript asking that a copy may be sent to a clergyman " directly," Shelley having " written to say it is coming." This I think almost positively implies that *Zastrozzi* was then published. Had it not been published, there would almost of a certainty have been a good deal about hurrying on the printer, binder, or publisher.

Whether the reviewers were " pouched," and if so what came of it, there is no evidence at present. If *The Critical Review* received a *douceur* from Almoner Graham, it was not taken kindly; for a two-page notice found by Professor Dowden in that review for November 1810 is anything but lenient in its tone towards the youthful romancist. The story and the style are characterized as " so truly contemptible that we should have passed it unnoticed had not our indignation been excited by the open and barefaced immorality and grossness displayed throughout." The virtuous reviewer was unable to say when he had " felt so much indignation as in the perusal of this execrable production. The author of it cannot be too severely reprobated. Not all his ' *scintillated eyes*,' his ' *battling emotions*,' his ' *frigorific torpidity* of despair,' nor his ' *Lethean torpor*,' with the rest of his nonsensical and stupid jargon, ought to save him from infamy and his volume from the flames."

Less than thirty years later a literary gentleman of mature years took so different a view of the matter that he reprinted the peccant volume in a collection, not of Shelley's works, but of novels and romances selected on their merits ; and *Zastrozzi* may be found figuring as the work of Shelley in No. 10 of *The Romancist, and Novelist's Library* (q.v.).

ORIGINAL POETRY BY VICTOR AND CAZIRE.

The second book of Shelley's whereof we have any trace is a volume of Poems of which no copy is at present forthcoming, but which certainly existed, and is pretty sure to come to the surface sooner or later. The fact that Shelley had issued in the Autumn of 1810 a volume entitled *Original Poetry by Victor and Cazire*, though made public in 1826, was not generally known to Shelley students until Mr. Garnett, having discovered it in

1859, made it known in June 1860 through *Macmillan's Magazine*. Numbers I to IX of *Stockdale's Budget* (13 December 1826 to 7 February 1827) contain a series of articles by Stockdale headed with Shelley's name. From the first of these it appears that, in the Autumn of 1810, Shelley called upon Mr. J. J. Stockdale, publisher, of Pall Mall, and arranged with him for the issue of a book printed at Horsham under the title quoted, and that, on the 17th of September 1810, Stockdale received 1480 copies of the book, "a thin royal 8vo. volume." Shelley is said to have been in a difficulty with the printer about the payment of the bill. The letters purporting to be from Shelley, published by Stockdale and republished by Mr. Garnett, are certainly genuine; for I have seen and carefully examined the original holographs; but only one of these letters is on the subject of the volume of poems, and that one does not give the title. It refers to the delivery of "the last proof impression" as having taken place on the 6th of September 1810 (see Prose Works, Volume III, page 331); so that we have it upon Shelley's own authority that the volume was set up in type, whatever may have been its subsequent fate. The book was advertized in *The Morning Chronicle* for the 18th of September 1810. The advertisement also appears in *The Morning Post* for the 19th of September and *The Times* for the 12th of October. The price of the book was 4*s*. There is every reason, *primâ facie*, for accepting Stockdale's reminiscences of Shelley as substantially true. The advertisements would be unlikely to represent a book only *going* to exist; and the fact that the volume was reviewed will probably be held to establish its existence conclusively. The following notice of it appeared in *The Poetical Register* for 1810-1811 (q.v.).

" *Original Poetry. By Victor and Cazire.* Small 8vo. pp. 64.

"There is no ' original *poetry* ' in this volume; there is nothing in it but downright scribble. It is really annoying to see the waste of paper which is made by such persons as the putters-together of these sixty-four pages. There is, however, one consolation for the critics, who are obliged to read all this sort of trash. It is, that the crime of publishing is generally followed by condign punishment, in the shape of bills from the stationer and printer, and in the chilling tones of the bookseller, when, to the questions of the anxious rhymer, how the book sells, he answers that not more than half a dozen copies have been sold."

Perhaps if this review were the only one in evidence it would be more circumspect to accept it as presumptive proof of the strongest kind in favour of the book's existence than to regard it as proof positive; for it is of course conceivable that the amount of circumstance which it contains was invented by some weary hack, reviewing books from a list of titles, and that some of those titles were only announced and never got affixed to real completed books. But those who have already been over-wearied with unearthed juvenilia of Shelley's must dismiss from their minds the solace derivable from this attitude of sceptical caution. Even if it were not unscientific, from a psychological point of view, to assume that Stockdale and the reviewer descended into the depths of almost aimless invention which would be implied, it would be preposterous to reject the review with extracts which Professor Dowden discovered in *The British Critic.* In that magazine for April 1811 occurs the following notice, which the wildest theorist on the side of non-existence must accept as demolishing the last hope that the *Original Poems of Victor and Cazire* never issued from the press at all :—

" When we ventured to say that poetical taste and genius abound in the present day, we by no means intended to assert, that we always meet with either the one or the other. Miserable, indeed, are the attempts which we are often doomed to encounter ; so miserable sometimes that it seems quite wonderful how any individuals fancying themselves able to write should be so far behind their contemporaries. One of the unknown authors of this volume begins by complaining, most sincerely, we are convinced, of the difficulty of writing grammatically, but there is another difficulty, which seems never to have entered the lady's head (if a lady !)—that is, the difficulty of writing *metrically.* In this she is still less successful than in the other, and does not seem at all to suspect it. The verse intended to be used is that of ' The Bath Guide,' and so it is *sometimes ;* but sometimes also not. For example—

' This they friendly will tell, and n'er make you blush,
With a jeering look, taunt, or an O fie ! tush !
Then straight all your thoughts in black and white put,
Not minding the *if's,* the *be's,* and the *but's.'*—P. 6.

Again :—

' My excuse shall be humble, and faithful, and true
Such as I fear can be made but by few.'—P. 7.

This *humble* and *faithful* lady lays claim *only* to ' sense, wit, and grammar ! ' Yet she tells her friend :—

> ' Be not a coward, *shrink* not a tense,
> But read it all over, *and make it out sense.*
> *What a tiresome girl !*—pray soon make an end.'—P. 9.

This last line, if not measure, contains at least truth in the first part, and a reasonable wish in the second.

" Two .epistles, in this exquisite style, begin the volume, which is filled up by songs of sentimental nonsense, and very absurd tales of horror. It is perfectly clear, therefore, that whatever we may say in favour of the poetry of this time, such volumes as this have no share in the commendation. One thing may be said in its favour, that the printer has done his task well; would he had been employed on something better ! If he has taste as well as skill, he must dread the names of Victor and Cazire."

According to Stockdale, about a hundred copies had been put into circulation, when he discovered in regard to some of the verses what the reviewer in *The Poetical Register* alleges of all, that they were not original. Shelley seems to have had a real collaborator ; and Stockdale found out that one of the poems (doubtless of " Cazire ") had already appeared as the work of M. G. Lewis. He communicated with Shelley, and the book was at once suppressed. Mr. Garnett conjectures that Cazire was the same colleague who is said to share with Shelley the glory of *Zastrozzi*, his cousin Harriet Grove. In default of the wording of the title-page, I give the *Morning Post* Advertisement:

(2)

This day is published, in royal 8vo., price 4s in boards,

ORIGINAL POETRY,

BY VICTOR AND CAZIRE,

Sold by Stockdale, Junior, No. 41, Pall Mall.

It will be observed that the missing book, though advertized and remembered by Stockdale as a *royal* octavo, is reviewed as a *small* octavo. People on the look-out for it must therefore not feel too sure as to the size. Sixty-four is most likely the right number of pages ; and the date on the title-page is in all probability 1811 ; for the criticisms of verse for 1810 in the volume of *The Poetical Register* referred to are separated from those for 1811 ; and the *Victor and Cazire* volume is noticed under 1811.

POSTHUMOUS FRAGMENTS OF MARGARET NICHOLSON.

This book is a quarto, consisting of fly-title, *Posthumous Fragments / of / Margaret Nicholson*, title, a third leaf bearing the "Advertisement," and text pages 7 to 29. At the foot of page 29 is the imprint *Munday, Printer, Oxford.* I suspect the work was issued as a stabbed pamphlet,—as the copies I have seen bear the usual traces of such issue. The title-page runs thus :—

(3)

POSTHUMOUS FRAGMENTS

OF

MARGARET NICHOLSON;

BEING POEMS FOUND AMONGST THE PAPERS OF THAT
NOTED FEMALE WHO ATTEMPTED THE LIFE
OF THE KING IN 1786.

EDITED BY

𝔍𝔒𝔥𝔫 𝔉𝔦𝔱𝔷𝔲𝔦𝔠𝔱𝔬𝔯.

OXFORD:
PRINTED AND SOLD BY J. MUNDAY.

1810.

A full account of this volume is to be found in Hogg's *Life of Shelley*, Volume I, pages 260 *et seq.* ; but it had already been inaccurately referred to by Medwin, both in *The Shelley Papers* and in his *Life of Shelley*. Hogg's account, written from memory, is certainly inaccurate in some points that can be checked by reference to the book itself; and this shows that his memory was not to be trusted implicitly. His talent for the picturesque, combined with this want of exactness, may easily have led him far from the facts, without any intention on his part to depart

from them. He relates that the poems were originally written
by Shelley *bonâ fide*, with the exception of the first, of which
"the MS. had been confided to Shelley by some rhymester of
the day,"—that Shelley showed the proof sheets of them to his
future biographer, and that the two friends eventually worked
upon them to make them into burlesques. When this was effec-
tually done, the printer, who was to have published the volume
at Shelley's cost, offered to do so at his own, and it was issued
under the name of the poor washerwoman who had attempted
the life of George III., and who was still alive, confined as a
lunatic during the pleasure of that monarch whom Shelley not
many years later described with tolerable accuracy as "An old,
mad, blind, despised, and dying king." So successful was the
hoax, says Hogg, that "we used to meet gownsmen in High-
street reading the goodly volume as they walked—pensive
with a grave and sage delight. . . . It was indeed a kind of
fashion to be seen reading it in public, as a mark of a nice dis-
cernment, of a delicate and fastidious taste in poetry, and the
very criterion of a choice spirit. Nobody suspected, or could
suspect, who was the author; the thing passed off as the
genuine production of the would-be regicide." It is, however,
to be noted that, in the contemporary letter from Oxford printed
in the *Diary Illustrative of the Times of George the Fourth* (q.v.),
the writer, who gives the common gossip of the University,
speaks of Shelley as having *published* this book, and evidently
understands it to be Shelley's own: he says "Shelley's style is
much like that of Moore burlesqued, for Frank is a very foul-
mouthed fellow, and Charlotte one of the most impudent brides
that I ever met with in a book"; and this clearly implies that
the writer considered the Epithalamium of François Ravaillac
and Charlotte Corday the production of Shelley and not of
Margaret Nicholson. I agree with Mr. Rossetti in thinking that
the traces of the process of burlesquing are not at all obvious.
The poems, with one exception, do not strike me as more ex-
travagant than others written by Shelley as a youth. If the account is correct, the first poem should keep its place in Shelley's
works for the sake of his share in burlesquing it: if incorrect, it
is as likely to be his own as the rest; and I must say that I think
it more likely that Shelley produced the whole volume except
that part of the Epithalamium of Ravaillac and Charlotte Corday
mentioned in the following letter, not, as far as I am aware,
published before,—a letter having a very curious bibliographical
interest, and not uninteresting on other grounds :—

Oxford Nov. 30 1810

My dear Graham

I enclose a 5£ note which is all I can immediately spare ; I shall see you in a fortnight.   Whenever you mention money make it *visible*, as since having looked over your letter I can find nothing like it.—The part of the Epithalamium which you mention, (i.e. from the end of Satan's triumph) is the pro-duction of a friend's *mistress* ; it had been concluded there, but she thought it abrupt and added this ; it is omitted in numbers of the copies,—that which I sent to my Mother of course did not contain it—I shall possibly send you the abuse to-day, but I am afraid that they will not insert it—But you mistake ; the Epi-thalamium will make it sell like wildfire, and as the *Nephew* is kept a profound secret, there can arise no danger from the in-delicacy of the Aunt—It sells wonderfully here, and is become the fashionable subject of discussion—What particular subject do you mean, I cannot make out I confess.—Of course to my Father Peg is a profound secret ; he is better and recovering very fast.—How is the King and what is thought of Political affairs.

Will you tell me what I owe you.

Yours affec[t]

P. B. Shelley

Although Mr. Slatter [1] of the firm of Munday & Slatter has recorded that the book was " almost still-born," it now appears that Shelley and Hogg are agreed in attributing to it a certain circulation ; and it may therefore be hoped that one of the castrated copies may yet come to light ; but I have never yet seen one.

I have only heard of four copies as extant at the present time ; and all of these contain the passage which the poet considered too indelicate for his mother's perusal, but which he seems to have relied upon as an incentive to buyers.   This letter lends no support to the participation of Hogg in the authorship ; and it seems likely enough that the contribution towards the ridiculous epithalamium is really the portion of the volume which Hogg had in his mind when he said the first poem was " confided to Shelley by some rhymester of the day."   The reference to certain abuse which Shelley might possibly send to Graham would amply suffice a blindly infuriated assailant, such as Shelley has been blessed withal, as foundation for a round

[1] Montgomery's *Oxford* (q.v.).

statement that the young Oxonian of eighteen years, whose ideas of literary morality were decidedly crude, had himself written an abusive notice of the indelicacy of the epithalamium, and only feared it might not be inserted in the newspaper to which he had communicated it; but such an interpretation of the sentence would be, to say the least, decidedly insecure.

Those who are sufficiently curious may learn something of the lunatic whose name served Shelley for a title, by consulting the *Life and Transactions of Margaret Nicholson, containing a Particular Account of her Attempt to Assassinate his Majesty; also Memoirs of her Remarkable Life, from Infancy to 9th August when she was conducted to Bedlam, by J. Fiske.* 1786. Among the curiosities of Shelleyan bibliography, it is amusing to note that a respectable London bookseller, desirous of conferring a fictitious value on this worthless volume, inserted in his catalogue, wherein £1 15s. was demanded for a copy, a note to the effect that "For editing the Posthumous Remains of Margaret Nicholson, the poet Shelley was expelled from Oxford,"—a statement worthy of Shelley's last assailant.

(4) Some years ago a so-called fac-simile of the *Posthumous Fragments* was issued without any intentional indication that it was not the original. But I presume it was executed from a much cut-down copy, for it is a considerably smaller quarto than the original. The same general particulars answer for the one book as for the other; but for the benefit of the unwary it may be set down that the paper of the reprint is thicker and stiffer than that of the original; that the two long rules in the title-page above and below the words *edited by John Fitzvictor* are straight rules in the reprint and fancy rules in the original; that at page 8 of the reprint, line 12, *baleful* is misprinted *hateful*; that in the heading of the poem beginning at page 11 the word *Ravaillac* is transferred in the reprint to the third line, being in the second in the original, and that the "French rules" which are of the plain form ——⬥—— in the original are of two less simple forms in the "fac-simile."

The only other separate issue of the *Posthumous Fragments* known to me is an octavo reprint, namely

(5)

POSTHUMOUS FRAGMENTS OF MARGARET NICHOL-SON./ EDITED BY H. BUXTON FORMAN,/ and printed for private distribution./ MDCCCLXXVII. .

This reprint consists of title as above, a second leaf bearing a bibliographical note, fly-title, title-page, and Advertisement as in the original, and pages 11 to 24 of text. The issue was restricted to 50 copies on ordinary paper, 25 on Whatman's hand-made paper, and 5 on vellum.

ST. IRVYNE.

St. Irvyne is a duodecimo volume consisting of fly-title, *St. Irvyne;/ or,/ the Rosicrucian,* with imprint at foot of the verso, *S. Gosnell, Printer, Little Queen Street, London,* title-page, and 236 pages of text, with head-lines throughout, *St. Irvyne; or,* on the left-hand, *the Rosicrucian* on the right.   At the foot of page 236 is the imprint *Printed by S. Gosnell, Little Queen Street, London.*   The title-page is as follows :—

(6)

ST. IRVYNE;

OR,

THE ROSICRUCIAN:

A ROMANCE.

BY

A GENTLEMAN

OF THE UNIVERSITY OF OXFORD

LONDON:
PRINTED FOR J. J. STOCKDALE,
41, PALL MALL.
1811.

In the letter of the 1st of April 1810, printed at page 5 of this volume, Shelley says that, if some one whom he designates as *Jock* (probably Robinson, the publisher of *Zastrozzi*) will not give him " a devil of a price " for his poem " and at least £60 " for his " New Romance in three volumes, the dog shall not have them."   Perhaps we may safely take this as a reference to *St. Irvyne,* and conclude that Mr. Robinson did not see his way to giving £60 for the book ultimately published by Stockdale under circumstances related in the series of articles discovered

by Mr. Garnett in *Stockdale's Budget* (q.v.). From one of
Shelley's letters in that publication, it seems that Stockdale was
at pains to " fit *St. Irvyne* for the press," Shelley being "by no
means a good hand at correction." On the 2nd of December
1810, Shelley wrote asking " When *does* ' St. Irvyne ' come
out ? " ; on the 18th of the same month he had seen Stockdale's
advertisement of it ; on the 20th he wrote to Hogg (Life,
Volume I, page 145), " *St. Irvyne* is come out; it is sent to you at
Mr. Dayrell's ; you can get one in London by mentioning my
name to Stockdale " ; on the 28th he wrote again (page 151),
" Your discrimination of that chapter is more just than the
praises which you bestow on so unconnected a thing as the
romance taken collectively " ; and on the 11th of January 1811
he had already had the bill for the printing, and was writing to
Stockdale to request that a copy of the book might be sent to
Harriett Westbrook. Mr. MacCarthy found, in *The Times* for
the 26th of January and 2nd of February 1811, an advertisement
of *St. Irvyne* opening with " *The University Romance.—This day
is published, price only 5s.* " ; and in *The British Critic* for the
same month Professor Dowden discovered a derisive notice of
the work.

(7) There seems to have been a remainder of the book
unsold in 1822 ; for copies are frequently found made
up from the original sheets, with a fresh title-page,
worded precisely as the original title-page is worded, but
with the date 1822. *St. Irvyne*, as well as *Zastrozzi*, was reprinted in *The Romancist* as the work of Shelley (in No. 60,
1840). I have never met with a *St. Irvyne* as made up in
1811, with a back label ; but the copies made up in 1822 have a
back label which reads " ST. IRVYNE ;/ OR, THE/ *Rosicrucian./*
A Romance./ Price 4s./ Boards./ 1822."

AN ESSAY ON LOVE.

(8) In a letter from Shelley to Godwin, headed "Keswick,
Jan. 16, 1812 ", and printed in Hogg's Life (Volume II,
pages 58-63) we read as follows : " I have desired the
publications of my early youth to be sent to you. You will
perceive that ' Zastrozzi ' and ' St. Irvyn ' [*sic*] were written
prior to my acquaintance with your writings—the ' Essay on
Love,' a little poem—since."

It is of course possible that, as suggested by Mr. MacCarthy, *An Essay on Love* is another name for *A Poetical Essay on the Existing State of Things* ; but it seems to me highly improbable ; and if it were the same, the second title would afford another reason for not confounding the book with a missing satire of 1811. It seems likely that *An Essay on Love* was one of the occasional trifles which " A Newspaper Editor " believed to have been printed at Horsham at the cost of Sir Bysshe.

LEONORA.

(9)   Another substantive work which was in all probability completed in manuscript, and almost entirely set up in type, was a novel entitled *Leonora*, said to have been written in conjunction with Thomas Jefferson Hogg. In the fourth edition of Robert Montgomery's *Oxford* (q.v.), in a " Biographical Summary of Eminent Characters connected with the University," occurs a most interesting communication from Mr. Henry Slatter, of the firm of Munday and Slatter. Among other details concerning Shelley, Mr. Slatter gave the following : —

" About this same period [1] he wrote a novel, (in conjunction, I have since learned, with Mr. Hogg, of the same college), entitled, ' Leonora,' which was commenced at the same press, but the printers refused to proceed with it, in consequence of discovering that he had interwoven his free notions throughout the work, and at the same time strongly endeavoured to dissuade him from its publication altogether ; but this was disregarded, and he afterwards took the copy to Mr. King, the printer, at Abingdon, who had nearly completed the work, but was stopped in its further progress, by the circumstance of Mr. Shelley's expulsion from Oxford, with his friend and associate Mr. Hogg."

Of so much of the work as was set up there would at all events have been a certain number of proof sheets ; and the chances are that the term " nearly completed " includes printing off the issue of the greater part of the sheets. This venture therefore probably represents a considerable mass of print and paper ; and it is by no means safe to assume that the book went completely out of existence when the Oxford catastrophe came.

[1] That is to say about the *Margaret Nicholson* period.

Book-hunters should be on the look-out for a book or portions of a book entitled *Leonora*, and should not disdain the linings of early nineteenth century trunks as mines of possible bibliographical wealth.

THE NECESSITY OF ATHEISM.

Shelley's next extant publication after *St. Irvyne* appears to be the tract which led to his expulsion from Oxford. It is a single foolscap sheet, folded in octavo, and consists of fly-title, 𝕿𝖍𝖊/ 𝕹𝖊𝖈𝖊𝖘𝖘𝖎𝖙𝖞 𝖔𝖋 𝕬𝖙𝖍𝖊𝖎𝖘𝖒, title-page as given below, a third leaf bearing the " Advertisement," the text occupying pages 7 to 13, and finally a blank leaf. The imprint at the end is *Phillips, Printers, Worthing.* There are no head-lines ; and the pages (8 to 13) are numbered centrally in Arabic figures.

(10)

THE

NECESSITY

OF

A T H E I S M.

———

Quod clarâ et perspicuâ demonstratione careat
pro vero habere mens omnino nequis humana.
Bacon de Augment. Scient.

———

WORTHING:
PRINTED BY E. & W. PHILLIPS.
Sold in London and Oxford.

There is much talk about this little work in the books of Hogg, Medwin, and others ; but it has not been generally known that any copy of it was extant. Some years ago I ascertained that the late Mr. Hookham had a copy bound up with other pamphlets by Shelley ; and from that copy, now in the possession of Sir Percy and Lady Shelley, the tract was reproduced in my edition. I have only succeeded in hearing of one other extant example ; but it was probably from neither of these that the tract was reviewed in 1822 in *The Brighton Magazine* (q.v.). Medwin says (*Life of Shelley*, Volume I, pages 139 *et seq.*) that *The Necessity of Atheism*

was " never offered for sale " : it was, he says, " a general issue,
a compendious denial of every allegation in order to put the
whole case in proof. ...   A formal mode of saying,—'You
affirm so and so,—then prove it.'...   But those who are anxious
to see this syllabus, may find it *totidem verbis* in the notes to
Queen Mab.   This syllabus he sent to me among many others,
and circulated it largely among the heads of colleges, and pro-
fessors of the university, forwarding copies it is said to several
of the bishops."   There are two inaccuracies here, at least : it
was offered for sale ; and the corresponding note to *Queen Mab*
(that on the words " There is no God ") varies much from the
tract in detail.   As to its being offered for sale, it is to be
observed that Mr. MacCarthy (see *Shelley's Early Life*, pagé
108) found in the *Oxford University and City Herald* of the 9th
of February 1811, under the words *Speedily will be published, to
be had of the Booksellers of London and Oxford*, the title of the
tract, and the motto from Bacon which turns out to be on its
title-page.

Moreover, Mr. Slatter's contribution to the Appendix to
Montgomery's *Oxford*, already mentioned, is conclusive and
unquestionable on this point.   The following extract on the
subject of the pamphlet leaves no possible doubt as to its having
been offered for sale ; and I have good authority for stating that
the period for which it was " on sale " at Munday and Slatter's
shop in Oxford was twenty minutes :—

"The pamphlet for which Mr. Shelley was expelled his
college was entitled ' The Necessity of Atheism,' and he himself
strewed the shop windows and counters of his booksellers in
Oxford, unknown to them, but gave instructions to their shop-
man to sell them as fast as he could and at the charge of sixpence each ; shortly afterwards a judicious friend of the booksellers, a fellow of a college, dropped in, and was attracted, by
the novelty of the title, to examine the contents of the pamphlet ;
he immediately desired to see one or both the principals, and at
once inveighed against the dangerous tendency of such a
pamphlet, and advised the destruction of them forthwith ; this
was immediately complied with, and they proceeded into a back
kitchen and burned them in this gentleman's presence ; at the
same time these booksellers sent a request to Mr. Shelley, to be
allowed a few minutes' conversation with him at their house ; he
came instanter, and it so happened that counsellor Clifford, of
O. P. notoriety, was in the house, and, being made acquainted
with the subject and at the earnest request of the booksellers,

undertook, in conjunction with the parties above-named, to use his best endeavours by entreaties, till entreaty seemed of no avail, and next by threats, to dissuade him from the error of his ways ; for the sake of himself, his friends, and connections ; all seemed of no avail—he appeared to glory in the course he had adopted, and said that he had sent a copy of his pamphlet to every bishop in the kingdom, to the Vice-Chancellor, and the other heads of houses in Oxford, and other dignitaries, addressing them under the fictitious signature of ' Jeremiah Stukeley.' "

Shelley's statement about the bishops may have been " brag." I do not think it was ; and it should at all events give us pause before dismissing as " transparently improbable or impossible " [1] Medwin's independent assertion that Shelley sent the pamphlet to the Bishops. The " fellow of a college " who " dropped in " is stated in a foot-note to have been the Rev. John Walker, B.C.L., fellow of New College, and afterwards vicar of Hornchurch, Essex, editor of " The Oxoniana " &c. It is well to be particular on this point, because this meddlesome gentleman may perhaps be regarded as a claimant to the honour of having denounced Shelley to the authorities of University College. Mr. Rossetti records that " A tutor of a different college is supposed to have denounced him." (Memoir, three volume edition, Volume I, page 23.)

Mr. Slatter's record has its bearing upon the probability of recovering further copies of *The Necessity of Atheism* ; and it must be borne in mind that Shelley sent one to Godwin later on, and therefore probably had some copies by him after he left the University. On the other hand, Mr. Slatter says his firm sent a friendly hint to Messrs. Phillips, the printers, " warning them of the dangerous tendency of disseminating such vile principles, and the liability they ran of a prosecution by the Attorney General, at the same time advising the destruction of every remaining copy, together with the MS. copy, types, &c." For the rest, as regards the considerable number of copies which probably got about, it must be remembered that the smallness of the tract rendered its existence peculiarly precarious.

[1] Mr. Rossetti adopts this sceptical attitude in the excellent memoir prefixed to his three volume edition (Volume I, page 22).

A POETICAL ESSAY ON THE EXISTING STATE OF THINGS.

A Poetical Essay on the Existing State of Things is said to have been published by Shelley for the benefit of Peter Finnerty, imprisoned for a libel on Castlereagh.   There is enough evidence of such a Poem having been published, to justify its insertion in a Shelley bibliography.   Personally, indeed, I do not doubt the existence of the book, or its authorship ; but as I conceive the laws of evidence, neither the one nor the other is proved.   It is to the late Mr. D. F. MacCarthy that we owe the discovery that such a book might be added to the catalogue of Shelley's writings ; and the main facts in evidence are of Mr. MacCarthy's finding, and are to be apprehended by a patient examination of his voluminous work *Shelley's Early Life* (q.v.).   No copy of the book is forthcoming ; but that fact goes for nothing.   That Shelley was interested in Finnerty is shown by the paragraph about that patriot and journalist in the *Address to the Irish People* (Prose Works, Volume I, page 352) ; but Mr. MacCarthy discovered that Shelley subscribed to a fund for Finnerty's benefit, the subscription being acknowledged in *The Oxford Herald* for the 2nd of March 1811 ; while, in the number for the 9th of March 1811, Mr. MacCarthy found the following advertisement " filling a space of about three inches, and printed in the most conspicuous part of the paper, at the head of the first column " :—

(11)

Literature.

Just published, Price Two Shillings,

A POETICAL ESSAY

ON THE

Existing State of Things.

AND FAMINE AT HER BIDDING WASTED WIDE
THE WRETCHED LAND, TILL IN THE PUBLIC WAY,
PROMISCUOUS WHERE THE DEAD AND DYING LAY,
DOGS FED ON HUMAN BONES IN THE OPEN LIGHT OF DAY.
Curse of Kehama.

BY A

GENTLEMAN of the University of Oxford.

For assisting to maintain in Prison

MR. PETER FINNERTY,

IMPRISONED FOR A LIBEL.

LONDON: SOLD BY B. CROSBY AND CO.,
AND ALL OTHER BOOKSELLERS.
1811.

There is no doubt that, while Shelley was in Dublin in March 1812, agitating for Catholic Emancipation &c., a notice of him appeared in *The Weekly Messenger*, a Dublin paper ; a letter from Shelley to Godwin published in Hogg's Life (Volume II, pages 90-5) refers to a newspaper as being sent to the philosopher with a copy of Shelley's second Irish Pamphlet on the 8th of March 1812 ; and in a postscript are the words " You will see the account of ME in the newspapers." Mr. MacCarthy showed that the newspaper sent *was* that which he found to contain an account of Shelley, for Godwin in reply quotes (Hogg's Life, Volume II, page 96) a passage from the *Proposals for an Association* as given in *The Weekly Messenger* ; but the fact that the poet sent the newspaper is hardly enough to authenticate, as Mr. MacCarthy contended, the Editor's statements about Shelley, one of which is as follows :—

" Mr. Shelley, commiserating the sufferings of our distinguished countryman Mr. Finnerty, whose exertions in the cause of political freedom he much admired, wrote a very beautiful poem, the profits of which we understand, from *undoubted* authority, Mr. Shelley remitted to Mr. Finnerty ; we have heard they amounted to nearly an hundred pounds."

The difficulty in regarding this as even approximate proof of the thesis maintained is enhanced by the consideration that, if the sale of the 2s. work were all profit, 1000 copies must be sold to produce £100. Moreover it should be obvious that other documents may exist undiscovered, other poems unadvertized, capable of throwing a different light on the affair ; and it is altogether hasty to assume as a proved and indisputable fact that the " very beautiful poem " was published or is identified. Mr. Rossetti, however, discovered and communicated to *The Academy* (19 December 1874) an additional statement of great value, and containing what seems to be an *insouciant* bungle, suggesting to the careful analyst at least authenticity. In the first volume of *A Diary illustrative of the Times of George the Fourth* (q.v.) there is a letter dated the 15th of March 1811, written from Christ Church, Oxford, detailing Shelley's doings. Here we read—

" Talking of books, we have lately had a literary Sun shine forth upon us here, before whom our former luminaries must hide their diminished heads—a Mr. Shelley, of University College, who lives upon arsenic, aqua-fortis, half-an-hour's sleep in the night, and is desperately in love with the memory of Margaret Nicholson. He hath published what he terms, the

Posthumous Poems, printed for the benefit of Mr. Peter Finnerty, which, I am grieved to say, though stuffed full of treason, is extremely dull, but the Author is a great genius, and if he be not clapped up in Bedlam or hanged, will certainly prove one of the sweetest swans on the tuneful margin of the Charwell . . . . Our Apollo next came out with a prose pamphlet in praise of atheism . . . . and there appeared a monstrous romance in one volume, called St. Ircoyne [*sic*], or the Rosicrucian. Shelley's last exhibition is a Poem on the State of Public Affairs."

In a later letter the writer, whom Mr. Rossetti identifies as Mr. Kirkpatrick Sharpe, mentions Shelley's expulsion. The degree of accuracy or the reverse seems to correspond well enough with the state of mind that would have mixed up the facts about the two poetical volumes; and the passages quoted form strong presumptive evidence that the Oxford advertisement of the *Poetical Essay* discovered by Mr. MacCarthy refers to the fourth of the books mentioned in the *Diary*. But it is right to mention that another Oxford authority, Mr. Slatter (see ante, pages 12 and 16) was under the impression that Shelley designed the profits of *Margaret Nicholson* for Finnerty. As Mr. Rossetti says (Poetical Works, 1878, Volume I, page 21), " it is difficult to doubt that a composition named *A Poetical Essay on the Existing State of Things* was actually published, and that the author of it was Shelley." The mention of this title in the " Catalogue " of *The Poetical Register* for 1810-1811 (q.v.) has no bearing on the question. Mr. MacCarthy conjectured that the poem would be satirical, and attempted to identify it with a missing satire of that period mentioned in Shelley's letters. It seems unlikely that the writer in *The Weekly Messenger* would call an early satire of Shelley's " a very beautiful poem "; and I shall presently have to consider the claims of a pamphlet to be regarded as the missing satire. To save the risk of disappointment in the *Poetical Essay*, let us clearly understand that, when that " very beautiful poem " does turn up, it will assuredly be found to be in the very beautiful taste of the eighteenth century—probably a little less hollow and trifling than the *Posthumous Fragments of Margaret Nicholson*, and somewhere midway between that level and the precarious altitudes of *Queen Mab*, wherein the still young muse of Shelley thought itself seriously occupied in the interests of posterity.

LINES ON A FÊTE AT CARLTON HOUSE.

(12) Mr. Rossetti in 1870, and again in 1878, published the following fragment taken down by Mr. Garnett " from the mouth of the Rev. Mr. Grove, a relative of Shelley," a fragment said to be all that Mr. Grove could recall of " a poem of about fifty lines which Shelley wrote and printed on a fête which had taken place towards the beginning of the summer of 1811." The fragment runs thus :

> By the mossy brink,
> With me the Prince shall sit and think ;
> Shall muse in visioned Regency,
> Rapt in bright dreams of dawning Royalty.

" A stream of water," says Mr. Rossetti, " had been made to meander down a long table ; and the extravagance of the affair generally had excited some murmurs. Shelley, it is said, ' amused himself with throwing copies of the poem into the carriages of persons going to Carlton House after the fête.' " It may be useful to add that, beside the expressions of dissatisfaction referred to above, there were at least two other poems on the subject. The first is probably well known to many people—*Carlton House Fête ; or, the Disappointed Bard &c. by Peter Pindar, Esq.*: in reviewing this *The Poetical Register* for 1810-11 (q.v.) speaks as if the matter were one of current ridicule. The other poem I find mentioned in the Catalogue of the same volume of the *Register,—The Regent's Fête or the Prince and his Country. By E. Fitzgerald, Esq.* Let us hope that some one who has saved these trifles for a " Regency " collection has also saved Shelley's leaflet or pamphlet, whichever it was.

THE MISSING SATIRE OF 1811.

In a letter to Hogg dated the 20th of December 1810, printed in Hogg's Life of Shelley, Volume I, pages 141-5, we read—" I am composing a *satirical* poem ; I shall print it at Oxford, unless I find, on visiting him, that R. is ripe for printing whatever will sell. In case of that, he is my man." " R." probably stands for Robinson, one of the publishers of *Zastrozzi*. Leigh Hunt says in his *Autobiography* that he "first saw Shelley during the early period of the *Examiner*, before its indictment on account of the Regent"; and against this passage Mr. Thornton Hunt noted in the edition of 1860 that it was "Mr. Rowland Hunter who first brought Leigh Hunt and his most valued friend personally together. Shelley had brought a manuscript poem which proved by no means suited to the publishing house in St. Paul's Churchyard [Mr. Hunter's]. But Mr. Hunter sent the young reformer to seek the counsel of Leigh Hunt." Assuming the son's interpolation into the father's Autobiography to be accurate, this first meeting must have taken place after the 2nd of March 1811, on which day Shelley in the express character of a stranger wrote to Hunt as editor of the *Examiner* (see Prose Works, Volume III, page 339). Let us suppose he had finished the satire he was writing at Christmas and was awaiting the result of negotiations with Robinson or some other bookseller. In the summer of 1811 came the Carlton House Fête, at the period of which we know he was in Town; and I think the allusions to a streamlet and a mossy bank (see page 23) indicate that that fête was fresh in his mind when he wrote the following undated letter now in the possession of Mr. F. Locker:

"If Graham, within that democratical bosom of thine, *yet* lingers a spark of loyalty, if a true and firm king's man ever found favour in thy sight, if thou art not totally hardened to streamlets, whose mossy banks invite the repose of the wanderer. . . .[1] If, I repeat, yet thou lovest thy rulers, and kissest the honeyed rod : :—Then, Graham do I conjure thee, by the great George our King, by our noble Prince Regent and our inimitable Commander in Chief then do I conjure thee by Mrs. Clarke, the Duke of Kent and Lord Castlereagh, together with Lord Grenville, that thou wilt assist me, (as heretofore thou didst promise) in my loyal endeavour to magnify, if magnification be possible, our Noble Royal Family. High let them soar . . . high as the expanse of the empyrean, and may no invidious louse dare to interrupt the reveries of frensied enthusiasm.—In fine, Græme, thou hast an harp of fire and I a pen of honey. Let then the song roll . . . wide let it roll . . . Take thou thy tuning fork . . . . for the ode is coming—lo ! Fargy thou art as the bard of old, I as the poet of other times . . . When kings murdered men; then was the lay of praise poured upon their

---

[1] These points are Shelley's and do not indicate omissions.

ears . . when adulation fled far, and truth, white robed seraph, descended to whisper into royal ears . . . They were not so rude as to say 'Thou Tyrant.' No! nor will I . . see if I do.

Philobasileus "

Outside the sheet is written the following stanza, already given in my edition of the Poetical Works (Volume IV, page 353), an effusion, by the bye, which, as Mr. J. MacCarthy writes to me to point out, is translated from the Marseillaise:

> Tremble Kings despised of man !
>   Ye traitors to your Country
> Tremble ! Your parricidal plan
>   At length shall meet its destiny . . .
> We all are soldiers fit to fight
> But if we sink in glory's night
> Our mother EARTH will give ye new
> The brilliant pathway to pursue
>   Which leads to DEATH or VICTORY . . .

Now one would suppose that the help for which Shelley was here appealing to Graham, who was clearly used to receiving appeals of this kind, was help to get a poem in praise of the Royal Family published ; and one knows that no such praise from Shelley would be other than ironical. That he had a poem to publish after March 1811 is clear, granting the accuracy of the Hunt evidence ; and what more natural than that he should appeal to his confidant Graham after Hunter's people had referred him to Hunt and Hunt had duly deprecated the publication of anything Shelley had written at that time, as Hunt infallibly would have done? Whoever knows the Shelley of that period will feel pretty sure that he got his satire published, so that there is nothing left to do but to find and identify it.

Some years ago, before I had any familiarity with the particulars set forth above, I found at a bookseller's shop a thin pamphlet which I picked out from a large number of such things because it commended itself to me as having the general air of a juvenile work of Shelley's. Careful examination of it has discovered so many points of contact with Shelley that I describe it here in the hope that someone may either bring forward other and better evidence of its being his, or such evidence of its being someone else's as will "put us to ignorance again " in regard to the missing satire of 1811. The title of my pamphlet runs thus :

(13)

LINES,

ADDRESSED

TO

HIS ROYAL HIGHNESS

THE

PRINCE OF WALES,

ON HIS

𝕭eing appointed 𝕽egent.

BY PHILOPATRIA, JUN.

SERUS IN CŒLUM REDEAS ; DIUQUE
LŒTUS INTERSIS POPULO QUIRINI.
Horace, Ode 2. Lib. 1̇.

LONDON :
PRINTED FOR SHERWOOD, NEELY, AND JONES,
PATERNOSTER-ROW ;
AND SOLD BY ALL OTHER BOOKSELLERS.

1811.

It is an octavo pamphlet consisting of title-page, 4 pages of Preface headed *To the Public*, with head-line *Address* and no numerals, and 18 pages of text containing fourteen lines in a full page. There is a pastoral-musical ornament at the head of page 1, repeated at the end of the poem. At the back of the title-page is the imprint *Hamelin and Seyfang, Printers, Queen Street, Cheapside.*

Concerning the title-page we have to note the resemblance between " Philopatria, Jun." and " Philobasileus," and the fact that the publishers are the same whose imprint afterwards appeared on the title-page of *Laon and Cythna.* Hamelin and Seyfang, I believe, were represented by Seyfang only in later years ; and C. F. Seyfang was the printer of *Swellfoot the Tyrant,* another Shelley pamphlet about George IV. The motto of Philopatria Junior shows that he had in mind, when writing these Lines to the Prince Regent, that ode to Octavianus Cæsar in which Horace set forth that in Octavianus only could the state hope for support, and in which he implored him to " seek his native skies late and live long among the people of Quirinus." Such is the line of ironical adulation taken by Philopatria Junior ; and such a composition might well be the " ode " with which Philobasileus threatened the devoted Graham.

AN ADDRESS TO THE IRISH PEOPLE.

An Address to the Irish People is a " stabbed " octavo pamphlet, consisting of title-page and 22 pages of text, including the post-script, which occupies the last leaf.   It is printed on three half-sheets, the title-page being the final leaf of the last half-sheet, and doubled back over the first two half-sheets. The pages have no head-lines, but are numbered centrally : and no printer's name appears.   The title-page runs thus :

(14)

AN ADDRESS,

TO THE

IRISH PEOPLE,

BY PERCY BYSSHE SHELLEY.

ADVERTISEMENT.

The lowest possible price is set on this publication, because it is the intention of the Author to awaken in the minds of the Irish poor, a knowledge of their real state, summarily pointing out the evils of that state, and suggesting rational means of remedy.—Catholic Emancipation, and a Repeal of the Union Act, (the latter, the most successful engine that England ever wielded over the misery of fallen Ireland,) being treated of in the following address, as grievances which unanimity and resolution may remove, and associations conducted with peaceable firmness, being earnestly recommended, as means for embodying that unanimity and firmness, which must finally be successful.

𝕯𝔲𝔟𝔩𝔦𝔫:

1812

Price—5d.

The type is exceedingly small and poor, and the paper very bad.   Though just double the length of the second Irish pamphlet it has only two more leaves.   The typography is moderately correct, though the punctuation, probably Shelley's, is eccentric.   In editing the Prose Works, I followed it rather than make and record innumerable small alterations, and I noted all those that it was absolutely necessary to make.   There is a copy in the British Museum.   Mr. MacCarthy, whose researches in the matter of the Irish Campaign are invaluable as to facts and details, fixed the date of publication of the *Address* as nearly as need be : he showed (*Shelley's Early Life*, pages 149 *et seq.*) that it came from the printer on the 24th of February 1812, that copies of it were sent to Godwin and Hamilton Rowan on that and the following day respectively, and that an advertisement appeared in *The Dublin Evening Post* of the 25th and 29th of February, and 3rd of March.

PROPOSALS FOR AN ASSOCIATION.

The *Proposals for an Association* appeared on Monday, the 2nd of March 1812, according to Mr. MacCarthy (*Shelley's Early Life*, page 172). It is an octavo pamphlet, consisting of title-page as given below, undated, and 18 pages of text, without head-lines, but numbered centrally.

(15)

PROPOSALS

FOR AN

A S S O C I A T I O N

OF THOSE

PHILANTHROPISTS,

WHO CONVINCED OF THE INADEQUACY OF THE MORAL AND POLITICAL STATE OF IRELAND TO PRODUCE BENEFITS WHICH ARE NEVERTHELESS ATTAINABLE ARE WILLING TO UNITE TO ACCOMPLISH ITS REGENERATION.

BY
PERCY BYSSHE SHELLEY.

Dublin:

PRINTED BY I. ETON, WINETAVERN-STREET.

The pamphlet is printed in the roughest style, with the worst possible ink, on the worst possible paper ; and many letters are dropped ; but it is not particularly incorrect, except in regard to the words *philanthropy, philanthropic,* &c., in which, oftener than not, there is an *h* after the *p* in the last syllable. Though these redundant aspirates were omitted in the reprint given in the Library Edition, I did not think it worth while to record the particular instances of correctness or the reverse, or to alter and record certain minor errors in grammar &c., for which

Shelley is probably responsible. The text was given from Lord Carlingford's copy, formerly in the collection of Sir Francis Freeling, who appears to have come into possession of it through his connexion with the Post Office espionage of which an account was given by Mr. MacCarthy. Stitched up with this copy are the original official correspondence relating to Shelley, and a copy of the Broadside *Declaration of Rights*.

DECLARATION OF RIGHTS.

(16) In addition to the two Irish pamphlets, Shelley appears to have got printed in Dublin the broadside entitled *Declaration of Rights*, which afterwards led to the imprisonment of his Irish servant Daniel Hill (or Healy) for uttering the same without an imprint. It is a roughly printed affair,— a single leaf measuring $14\frac{7}{8}$ inches by $8\frac{15}{16}$ inches. Although this curious document was reprinted by Richard Carlile in *The Republican* for the 24th of September 1819 (q.v.), and figures in Lowndes's Bibliographer's Manual (Bohn's edition, page 2374) as having occurred in a certain copy of *Queen Mab* not now forthcoming, it remained for Mr. Rossetti to place it before the present generation of Shelley's readers in an article contributed to *The Fortnightly Review* for January 1871, entitled "Shelley in 1812-13." Mr. Rossetti (page 71) points out the resemblances between this Declaration and two such Documents of the French Revolution, "the one adopted by the Constituent Assembly in August, 1789, and the other proposed in April, 1793, by Robespierre." Mr. MacCarthy (*Shelley's Early Life*, page 323) called attention to the recurrence, in the *Declaration of Rights*, of certain thoughts and phrases from the *Proposals for an Association*. For a concise account of Shelley's proceedings at Barnstaple with this hand-bill, see page 37 of the memoir prefixed to Volume I of Mr. Rossetti's edition of Shelley's Poetical Works (3 volumes, 1878). There are two copies of the Broadside preserved in the Public Record Office ; and Lord Carlingford has the copy sent officially to Mr. (afterwards Sir Francis) Freeling, Secretary of the Post Office, by the Post Office Agent at Holyhead, under circumstances fully detailed by Mr. MacCarthy (*Shelley's Early Life*, pages 309 *et seq.*). By his Lordship's courtesy, the text was given in the Library Edition from that copy.

In collating the broadside *Declaration* with the reprint in *The Republican* for the 24th of September 1819, I have only found a single verbal variation, an evident misprint, *we* for *they*, in the third line of article 26.   The punctuation is also practically the same.   We shall perhaps never know whether Shelley furnished Carlile with the copy of the broadside from which the reprint was made; but it is not impossible,—scarcely improbable, as the poet had certainly a feeling of friendly interest in the more daringly practical agitator, which friendly interest was reciprocal.   For, on the one hand, in a letter headed *Florence, Nov. 6, 1819* (Prose Works, Volume IV, page 138), Shelley says he has "just finished a letter of five sheets on Carlile's affair" (a prosecution for selling books called irreligious) ; and, on the other hand, the fourteen volumes of *The Republican* contain a number of laudatory articles on and friendly references to Shelley.   In the same number with the *Declaration of Rights* is a rashly outspoken letter from Carlile to the Prince Regent, "On his answer to the Address and Petition of the Citizens of London, in Common Council assembled, praying his Royal Highness to institute an enquiry into the conduct of the Magistrates and Yeomanry Cavalry of Manchester,"—on the occasion of the "massacre" which inspired Shelley to write *The Mask of Anarchy.*   The *Declaration* is followed in *The Republican* by three abstracts of "Benefits," which are extremely well set forth, and might or might not be memoranda of Shelley's for his still unpublished treatise on Reform.   The first of these abstracts is headed "BENEFITS OF THE REVOLUTION IN FRANCE, *Concerning which it is presumed few will disagree.*" The second is headed "OTHER BRANCHES OF REFORM, *Concerning which it is presumed a great part of the consistent Friends of Freedom and of Human Happiness will be agreed.*"   The third is headed "*Benefits likely to accrue from a Reform in the House of Commons, or properly speaking, a Revolution in the Affairs of Great Britain and Ireland.*"   These notes do not appear to be connected with Shelley's Irish Campaign ; but, if his, might have been sent to Carlile with a copy of the *Declaration*, which was appropriate enough to the political situation.

THE DEVIL'S WALK.

(17) *The Devil's Walk, a Ballad,* published by Shelley in 1812, is a broadside measuring $18\frac{1}{8}$ by $14\frac{1}{2}$ inches: the ballad is printed in three columns, divided into stanzas as shown in my edition, but without numerals, which I added for convenience of reference. The title is in large old-English characters. The poem did not become generally known (indeed I do not know of any living person having heard of it) until Mr. Rossetti reprinted it in a valuable article entitled "Shelley in 1812-13," which appeared in *The Fortnightly Review* for January 1, 1871 (q.v.). The circumstances under which the only copy of the broadside I have heard of as now extant got preserved, and eventually filed in the Public Record Office, form an important episode in the early career of Shelley. It is sufficient to state here that the original broadside was distributed together with the *Declaration of Rights,* with the aid of Shelley's servant, Daniel Hill (or Healy), and a curious machinery of boxes and bottles for marine service, about the shores of North Devon. Shelley was living at Lynmouth at the time; but it was at Barnstaple that Daniel Hill was apprehended, convicted of distributing printed papers with no printer's name on them, and imprisoned. This poem of *The Devil's Walk* is by no means unimportant as a land-mark in the history of Shelley's poetic developement; and, as the honour of unearthing it belongs to Mr. Rossetti, I can do no better than quote the following remarks from his article. "Many readers will remember that there is a poem by Southey named *The Devil's Walk,* and also a poem by Coleridge named *The Devil's Thoughts,* the two being to a great extent identical. The original authorship of this joint composition has been much discussed; one statement is that Porson was the real inventor. However, I suppose that Southey's distinct assertion ought to be accepted : Southey himself started the idea, and wrote the larger part of the poem, in 1799 ; Coleridge wrote various stanzas ; Porson had nothing to do with it. Shelley's poem is obviously, undisguisedly, founded on that of Southey and Coleridge: he has borrowed the idea, and written a different composition to develop it. There is only one stanza (that which begins ' Satan saw a lawyer a viper slay ') that is directly appropriated from the earlier work,—as I gather, from Coleridge's portion of it ; and

even this is differently worded. Coleridge's production, read apart from Southey's, is no doubt better than Shelley's; but I think Shelley's compares creditably with the completed joint original. There are certainly some good points in his *Devil's Walk*; and it may safely receive this extremely qualified meed of praise, that it is the best now extant piece of poetry produced by the future author of *Prometheus Unbound* prior to the printing of *Queen Mab* (1813)."

A LETTER TO LORD ELLENBOROUGH.

A Letter to Lord Ellenborough is a small octavo, or large old-fashioned duodecimo: I cannot say which, for there are no signatures to mark the sheets, and Lady Shelley's copy, the only one I have seen, is bound up in one precious volume with *The Necessity of Atheism* and the two Irish pamphlets. It consists of title-page as given below, Advertisement on a second leaf, and pages 1 to 23 of text, without head-lines, numbered centrally with Arabic figures in square brackets. It bears no printer's name.

(18)

A LETTER

TO

LORD ELLENBOROUGH,

Occasioned by the Sentence which he passed on

Mᴿ D. I. EATON,

As Publisher of

The THIRD PART of PAINE's AGE OF REASON.

Deorum offensa, Diis curæ.

—It is contrary to the mild spirit of the Christian Religion, for no sanction can be found under that dispensation which will warrant a Government to impose disabilities and penalties upon any man, on account of his religious opinions. [*Hear, Hear.*]

Marquis Wellesley's Speech. Globe, July 2.

In a letter to Godwin dated " Cwm-Rhayader, June 11, 1812 " (Hogg's Life, Volume II, page 129), Shelley writes thus : " What do you think of Eaton's trial and sentence ? I mean not to insinuate that this poor bookseller has any characteristics in common with Socrates, or Jesus Christ, still the spirit which pillories and imprisons him, is the same which brought them to an untimely end—still, even in this enlightened age, the moralist and reformer may expect coercion analogous to that used with the humble yet zealous imitator of their endeavours. I have thought of addressing the public on the subject, and indeed have begun an outline of the address. May I be favoured with your remarks on it before I send it to the world ?" By the 29th of July the essay on this subject seems to have been written and printed. Hogg (Volume II, page 152) represents Shelley as writing on that date that it had been printed in London ; but without seeing Shelley's letter we cannot be sure of the precise bearing of his words. Mr. J. R. Chanter, in *Sketches of the Literary History of Barnstaple* (1866, page 55) gives a circumstantial account of the printing of the tract by Mr. Syle of Barnstaple ; and Mr. MacCarthy (*Shelley's Early Life*, page 345) accepts this statement. The greater part of the edition of *A Letter to Lord Ellenborough* is said to have been destroyed by Mr. Syle on his observing the nature of it ; but fifty copies were sent to Mr. Hookham of Bond Street ; and Mr. Chanter says that they were distributed and could not be got back. Their transmission is mentioned in Shelley's letter to Hookham of the 18th of August 1812 (*Shelley Memorials*, page 38) ; and it was from a copy of the pamphlet preserved by Hookham that Lady Shelley reprinted in the *Memorials* those portions which, being personal to Mr. Eaton and Lord Ellenborough, had not already been reprinted in the note on the words *I will beget a Son* in *Queen Mab*. From the same copy, by the kindness of Sir Percy and Lady Shelley, the pamphlet was given in its integrity in the Library Edition. Some very trenchant passages were out of currency from 1812 till 1880. As in the case of *The Necessity of Atheism*, Shelley revised his work when inserting it in *Queen Mab*.

An abridged edition of the Letter, reprinted from the *Shelley Memorials*, appeared in New York in 1879 as No. 156 of the " Truth Seeker Tracts." It consists of six leaves sewn together, without title-page or wrapper, but headed thus :—

(19)

Free Speech and Free Press./ BY PERCY BYSSHE SHELLEY./ A LETTER TO LORD ELLENBOROUGH OCCA-SIONED BY/ A SENTENCE PASSED BY HIM UPON MR. J. D./ EATON FOR PUBLISHING PART THIRD OF PAINE'S/ "AGE OF REASON" ABOUT THE YEAR 1812./ [*Dedicated to Judge Benedict*]

Mr. R. Forder, to whom I am indebted for this tract, tells me that the occasion of its issue was the imprisonment in 1879 of Mr. D. M. Bennett, Editor of *The New York Truth-seeker*, who was sentenced by Judge Benedict to thirteen months' imprisonment, served eleven, was afterwards sent on a voyage round the world by the free-thinkers of America, was fêted in London at the Hall of Science in September 1881, arrived home in October 1882, and died suddenly a few days after his return.   My informant says the tract had an immense sale in the United States and Canada, and that Col. Knox-Browne of Texas spent a thousand dollars in copies which he gave away in most of the principal cities of the States.

In 1883 the complete Letter was reproduced from my edition as a separate pamphlet, with the following title:—

(20)

SHELLEY/ ON/ BLASPHEMY./ BEING HIS/ 𝕷etter to 𝕷ord 𝕰llenborough,/ OCCASIONED BY THE/ Sentence which he passed on Mr. D. I. EATON,/ as Publisher of the Third Part of/ PAINE'S "AGE OF REASON."/ *PRICE ONE PENNY.*/ LONDON:/ PROGRESSIVE PUBLISHING COMPANY,/ 28 STONECUTTER STREET, E.C./ 1883.

This is a single sheet folded in eight, without wrapper.   On the verso of the title-page is Shelley's Advertisement.   A short "Introduction" begins on page 3 and ends on page 5, where the Letter commences.   At page 8 is a foot-note signed "J. M. W." (Joseph Mazzini Wheeler).   The Letter ends on page 14. Page 15 is occupied by the lines "Think not the tyrants will rule for ever," &c., and the imprint of the Company ; and at page 16 are advertisements of Mr. G. W. Foote's publications.

QUEEN MAB.

The *editio princeps* of *Queen Mab* is a crown octavo volume consisting of title-page, Dedication, pages 1 to 122 of text, fly-title *Notes*, and pages 125 to 240 of Notes. I never saw a copy with a printed label, and have no reason to think there was one. The title-page runs thus:

(21)

QUEEN MAB;

A

PHILOSOPHICAL POEM:

WITH NOTES.

BY

PERCY BYSSHE SHELLEY.

ECRASEZ L'INFAME!
Correspondance de Voltaire.

Avia Pieridum peragro loca, nullius ante
Trita solo; juvat integros accedere fonteis;
Atque haurire: juratque novos decerpere flores.
     *   *   *   *   *
Unde prius nulli velarint tempora musæ.
Primum quod magnis doceo de rebus; et arctis
Religionum animos nodis exsolvere pergo.
Lucret. lib. iv.

Δος πε ςῶ, καὶ κοσμον κινησω.
Archimedes.

LONDON:
PRINTED BY P. B. SHELLEY,
23, Chapel Street, Grosvenor Square.
1813.

In a letter to Mr. Thomas Hookham, dated the 18th of August 1812, Shelley says "I enclose also, by way of specimen, all that I have written of a little poem begun since my arrival in England. I conceive I have matter enough for six more cantos. You will perceive that I have not attempted to temper my constitutional enthusiasm in that poem. Indeed, a poem is safe; the iron-souled Attorney-General would scarcely dare to attack. The Past, the Present, and the Future, are the grand and comprehensive topics of this poem. I have not yet half exhausted the second of them." The editor of the *Shelley Memorials*, wherein, at page 39, this passage occurs, says "The poem here alluded to is (I conceive) *Queen Mab.*" This assumption is almost certainly correct; for, even if we may trust that statement of Medwin (*Life of Shelley*, Volume I, page 153) which carries the commencement of the composition as far back as the autumn of 1809, we may be quite certain that anything sketched by Shelley in 1809 and resumed in 1812 would be entirely rewritten; and he might naturally speak of it as a newly-commenced work. The poem was finished in February 1813; and the notes were put together after that date. He did not publish the book in the usual way, but printed it privately. I should say the errors and irregularities of the press were comparatively few. The book was printed on fine paper, in the belief that, though it would not be read by the aristocrats of that day, it might be by their sons and daughters; and the chances are that not a copy, of the 250 said to have been printed, was wasted. Carlile, one of the numerous publishers of piratical editions of *Queen Mab*, affords us a curious piece of evidence on this point: an advertisement was issued by this man in *The Republican* in 1822, shortly after Shelley's death, to the effect that he had on sale, with his own edition of *Queen Mab*, 180 copies of Shelley's edition; and, looking at the rapidity with which pirated editions followed Carlile's, I should not doubt that he got rid of all of his.

In the *Alastor* volume, it will be remembered, Shelley published *The Dœmon of the World, a Fragment*,—a very much altered version of the first two Cantos of *Queen Mab*. This altered version he completed by a similar revision of the last two Cantos, as " Part II." The two parts show pretty clearly what the mature Shelley of 1815 considered worth preserving of *Queen Mab*; and it seemed to me when editing the poems far better to introduce Part II among the mature works than to give it in the form of extensive notes along with the immature *Queen Mab*, in the appendix of *juvenilia*. Indeed, no ordinary reader could form an idea of the scope of *The Dœmon of the World* if it were left to be picked out from notes, however carefully those might be framed with a view to facilitate this operation; and only a few students would find time to reconstruct the poem in imagination.

The revised copy of *Queen Mab* from which the complement

of *The Dæmon of the World* was given in my edition lay *perdu* for nearly twenty years. It was mentioned by Medwin as long ago as 1847, in the first volume of his *Life of Shelley* (pages 101 *et seq.*) ; and some further account of it appeared in Middleton's *Shelley and his Writings* in 1858. Medwin refers to it as in the possession of Mr. Brooks, who reissued several of Shelley's works : " He had," says Medwin, " a correspondent at Marlow, who knew Shelley, . . . from whom he obtained a copy of *Queen Mab*, which, like *The Wandering Jew*, had probably been left by Shelley's inadvertence in his abode there. This copy was exceedingly interlined, very much curtailed and modified, as by a specimen given in a fragment entitled *The Dæmon of the World* appended to *Alastor* ; and what is still more important and worthy of remark, with the Notes torn out. This copy had been revised with great care, and as though Shelley had an intention at the time of bringing out a new edition, an idea which his neglect of his labour shews he soon abandoned. This emendated work is a great curiosity, and has scattered about the pages rude pen-and-ink drawings of the most fantastic kind, proving the abstraction of his mind during this pursuit . . . . That Mr. Brooks (he was the publisher if not the printer of the Owenites) did not make use of the *refacciamenti* or *pentimate* [*sic*] in his reprints of *Queen Mab*, may easily be conceived, for these very alterations were the only objectionable parts to him, and he would have thought it a sacrifice to have struck out a word of the original text, much less the notes. *Queen Mab* is indeed the gospel of the sect, and one of them told me that he had found a passage in Scripture, that unquestionably applied to Shelley, and that the word *Shiloh* was pronounced in the Hebrew precisely in the same manner as his name."

Middleton says in his preface, " Captain Medwin, who was aware of the existence of the volume revised and corrected by Shelley himself, appears to have been but imperfectly acquainted with it. I have been enabled to supply a deficiency in this respect, and the specimens given will convey a favourable idea of the value of the whole." As will be presently apparent, Middleton himself was in 1858 either " but imperfectly acquainted " with the book, and also with the intentions of its owner,—or desirous of keeping the public ill-informed on the subject. He announced in a foot-note that " a new edition of *Queen Mab*, with Shelley's own revisions," was " preparing for the Press"; but no such edition has yet, I believe, been published. His account of the discovery of the volume is a mystified reproduction of Medwin's account. "The volume which Shelley revised," says Middleton, "and enriched with many additions and corrections, was left at Marlow, where it had been thrown aside, and, no doubt, forgotten, among the many anxieties he was there subject to. It fell afterwards into the hands of a gentleman attached to the Owenites, and has been ever since carefully concealed from the eyes of the world. As the poem stands in the original, its doctrines exactly accord with their tenets, and it is to a considerable extent the gospel of the Owenites, while these revisions and erasures would have produced it in a very modified form."

Middleton collated four passages of the *Dæmon of the World* fragment (in the *Alastor* volume) with the corresponding passages in *Queen Mab*, italicizing the variations (and these passages show one or two verbal variations that are not in the fragment and are in the book); he printed three lines which he described as being introduced into the "conclusion of the fourth division of the poem," though they really happen to be the three clearest lines of a rather complicated interpolation for the opening of the fifth division, written in the convenient blank half-page facing that opening; and he quoted two other manuscript variations of three lines each,—one for the fifth and one for the ninth section. Thus, as Part I of *The Dæmon of the World* was already published by Shelley himself, the public was indebted to Middleton for nine lines of *variorum* readings. It is curious to find the revisions given by Middleton differing occasionally from both the *Alastor* version and that of the revised *Queen Mab*. For instance the passage which in *Queen Mab* stands thus ‹

> The other, rosy as the morn
> When throned on ocean's wave
> It blushes o'er the world :
> Yet both so passing wonderful !

is said by Middleton to be remodelled into

> The other, glowing like the vital day
> When, throned on ocean's wave
> It blushes o'er the world ;
> Yet both so strange and wonderful.

Now the first line as altered in pencil in the book can be so made out, though Shelley eventually printed

> The other glowing like the vital *morn*
> When throned on ocean's wave
> It *breathes over* the world
> Yet both so *passing strange and* wonderful.

The word *breathes* is also plainly written in the revised book
and *blushes* plainly cancelled; but the cancelling of *o'er* and
writing of *over* are very faint. There is a *caret* between *passing*
and *wonderful,* no word marked out in that line, but the word
dark written in the margin, and struck out again, another word
being put beside it, which is unintelligible, but is certainly not
the word *strange.* The inference seems to me to be that Middleton had had very limited access both to this book and to the
Alastor volume; for how can he have got the word *strange* but
from that, or *the vital day* but from this? Later on, he says the
line

> From the celestial hoofs,

(by the bye, he says *hoof*) is altered to

> From the celestial *pinions,*

and so it is in the revised book, plainly, in ink; whereas in the
Alastor volume we have

> From the swift sweep of wings.

If on one occasion he had jotted down, in a copy of *Queen Mab,*
some of the revisions in this book, and on another some of those
in the *Alastor* volume, he might easily have got such a result as
we find, when he came to make up his notes for a parade of
variations shown by the book. Referring to the passages he
quotes, he says,—" These I only give as specimens of the revisions contained in this curious volume. It is evident from
their variety and the nature of them, that Shelley had gone
carefully through the poem; and it is to be regretted that he did
not publish it in the form his riper judgment and discrimination
would have approved of; but two years later he seems to have
entertained the idea of entirely remodelling the poem in the
form of the regular rhyming stanza of octosyllabic verse; an
idea which, from the specimen given in Mrs. Shelley's notes of
the Invocation to the Soul of Ianthe, the reader will observe it
is by no means to be regretted he did not accomplish." It is
here to be remarked that the expression " two years later "
seems to imply that the revisions were made in 1813; indeed
Middleton says "no sooner was this volume printed than he
began to waver in his notions concerning it, and industriously
sat down to the work of revision"; but no authority for this
statement is adduced beyond the fact of a copy having been revised; and I think it most unlikely that the revisions were of
an earlier date than 1815. Thus the idea that Shelley ever

thought of doing the whole poem in rhyming stanzas may be dismissed as an assumption of Middleton's based upon a fictitious dissociation of the Dæmon's Invocation[1] from the rest of the revisions. Mrs. Shelley, in her note on *Queen Mab*, says, " a few years after, *when printing Alastor*, he extracted a small portion which he entitled ' The Dæmon of the World ; ' in this he changed somewhat the versification—and made other alterations scarcely to be called improvements. I extract the invocation of Queen Mab to the Soul of Ianthe, as altered in ' The Dæmon of the World.' I give it as a specimen of the alterations made." This has always seemed to me to fix the date of the revision as 1815.

This superficial acquaintance of Middleton's with the bearings of Mrs. Shelley's note corresponds precisely with a very meagre acquaintance with the revised book about which he makes so much parade to such small result ; and, in support of my suspicion that he had only been able to make an inspection of the most cursory kind, I may observe that two of the three-line specimens which he quotes from the emendations are written prominently and clearly, and that the third, which is a little difficult to make out (but certainly not more difficult than the passages from the *Alastor* volume given as from the revised copy of *Queen Mab*) is not only imperfect, but incorrect even as far as it goes. I think that, if Mr. Brooks held the views attributed to him by both Medwin and Middleton, he would not have been likely at that time to let Middleton see much of the book ; and that he was the " gentleman attached to the Owenites," whose name is so carefully concealed by the later biographer, is sufficiently evidenced by the fact that the book was still in his hands in or about 1870, when he gave it to an enthusiastic lover and indeed disciple[2] of Shelley's. Eventually, however, Middleton must have had the book at his disposal ; for a copy exists with the manuscript markings carefully transcribed, apparently by

---

[1] Pages 63-4, Volume I, of my edition.

[2] This was Thomas Wade, the author of *Mundi et Cordis Carmina* and numerous other admirable works, through the greater part of which there runs a clear note of Shelley's influence. His most beautiful poem is perhaps *The Contention of Death and Love*, written upon the text, from *Laon and Cythna*,

I am worn away
And Death and Love are still contending for their prey.

Wade died in 1875, after a literary career of half a century, concerning which so little is generally known, that he certainly ranks among " the inheritors of unfulfilled renown." It was by the great kindness of his widow (since deceased) that I was enabled to give the public the benefit of this long-hidden book.

him ; but this may just as well have been done after the issue of *Shelley and his Writings* as before. If before, we are almost bound to assume " malice prepense " instead of ignorance as the explanation of his inaccuracy ; and I do not lean towards malice prepense in his case or Medwin's.

Until the actual book worked upon by Shelley came into my hands I was never wholly satisfied that there were not two revised copies of *Queen Mab* in question, one seen by Medwin and one by Middleton,—a doubt which of course involved the suspicion that Middleton was under a misapprehension as to the identity of the copy he saw with that which Medwin saw. Medwin could not remember the name of the gentleman from whom Mr. Brooks had the book ; and Middleton, though giving that, concealed Mr. Brooks's name ; but, as there is no conceivable reason for doubting that Medwin really refers to the copy in the hands of Mr. Brooks (about whom his statements are very circumstantial), and as the copy lying before me as I write is unquestionably the one Middleton saw, I think it follows as a matter of course that there really was but one copy in question. The absolute certainty that this is the copy referred to by Middleton rests principally on a very curious detail : the revisions for the *Dœmon of the World* fragment in the *Alastor* volume form no positive identification, although they are strongly in favour of the identity,—and the other three variations given by Middleton might have been written by Shelley in more copies than one, though they were not likely to be copied as exactly as the correspondence of Middleton's extracts with the book would indicate ; but Middleton says : " At the conclusion of the fourth division of the poem, some additional lines are introduced—

> ' The buds unfold more brightly, till no more
> Or frost, or shower, or change of seasons mar
> The freshness of its amaranthine leaves.'

And underneath the last line are written the words α μαραινω, which might lead us to suppose that while the poet was composing the line he was musing over the Greek derivation of the word amaranthine." I turn to the revised book and find the Greek words written precisely in the place indicated. I am strongly impressed with the belief that Middleton's first knowledge of the book's existence was derived from Medwin, and that it was through reading Medwin's Life that he was induced to seek out Mr. Brooks.

As regards the discrepancies between Medwin's description

and the facts of the book lying before me, I can only say they
are highly characteristic of Medwin's whole work, which I have
no doubt is meant for true, but which is one of the least accurate
books ever published. He says the notes were torn out of the
copy he describes; and we find the notes here, but without a
single mark upon them: he says the book "has *scattered about
the pages* rude pen-and-ink drawings of the most fantastic kind;"
and we find one side of the cover decorated in this way, and one
page ornamented with four grotesque faces, scrawled with a pen
and ink between and among some lines of fresh verse written for
The Dæmon of the World. These variations of description and
fact go for nothing, in the circumstances of the case: supposing
the book before me to be the one described, the account is pretty
accurate for Medwin,—who may easily have forgotten whether
the notes were ignored by excision or by simply being left alone,
and would be most unlikely to have more than a vague notion of
the pen-and-ink scribblings. I take it, therefore, for almost
a certainty that the book mentioned by Middleton, and now
under description, is as Middleton stated, the one described by
Medwin.

There is still one point on which I feel some doubt: both
biographers are agreed in stating that the book was got by Mr.
Brooks from a gentleman at Marlow who came by it accidentally:
Mrs. Wade, on the other hand, told me that when Mr. Brooks
gave it to Wade, he stated that it had been given to him by
Shelley; and that Shelley really did give it away is to some
extent implied by its having the usual mutilations. It is well
known that when Shelley gave away copies of *Queen Mab* he removed the title-page, the dedication to Harriett, and the imprint
at the end of the volume; and from this revised copy, these
portions are cut out with a knife according to his fashion. I do
not see why he should have removed them if he were going to
keep the book.

The first point of interest is found inside the cover, where
Shelley has written, in pencil, *The Queen of the Universe*, as if he
had some idea of re-christening his poem by that name: underneath are written, also in pencil, the words *the metre—Pastor
Fido*,—evidently a memorandum for that passage in the preface
to *Alastor* &c., wherein he describes the metre of *The Dæmon of
the World* as being "that of Samson Agonistes and the Italian
pastoral drama." This detail is of consequence as hinting that
this copy was really in use by Shelley while he was getting out
the *Alastor* volume.

The first two sections show many of the copious revisions made for the *Dæmon of the World* fragment published in that volume,—some in pencil, some in ink; and there are of course cancelled readings. It is to be remarked that the rhymed Invocation of the Dæmon is wanting; but, as there are some pin-holes in this part of the book, I have no doubt the Invocation was written on a separate sheet (indeed there was no room to write it in the margins) and finally detached for printer's copy, when the fragment went to press as part of the *Alastor* volume.

The third section is untouched: the fourth has seven lines cancelled, but nothing written in their place: the first page of the fifth is much revised and interpolated, but the rest untouched: the sixth contains the revision of a line and a half for the passage which was detached under the title of *Superstition* and published with *Alastor*,[1] but no further change; and the seventh is intact. The eighth and ninth sections contain the important revisions and interpolations for the Second Part of *The Dæmon of the World*, first published in the third volume of my edition; and there are also alterations in passages that were after all rejected from the revised poem: these appear in *variorum* notes to *Queen Mab* in the fourth volume of my edition. Shelley's way of indicating the transpositions that form a part of the revision was not very easy to fathom, though secure enough when found out; and it would be impossible to describe it clearly.

The only remaining peculiarity of this copy is a sum done in pencil on the fly-title to the Notes; but even so small a matter as a sum in simple multiplication may be psychologically interesting. The one in question is a multiplication of 122 by 21; and the correct result is duly arrived at. Shelley evidently wanted to know about how many thousand lines *Queen Mab* contained; and his method of approaching that knowledge was characteristically inexact. The poem ends on page 122: the full page contains 22 lines: a page with one space before a new paragraph contains 21 lines; and Shelley would seem to have accepted that as the average,—leaving out of consideration the eighteen opening and concluding pages, four entirely blank pages occurring when the section chances to end on a recto, and the numerous instances in which the number of lines in a page is reduced below 21 by multiplication of spaces.

It is also worth recording, as characteristic of another mental

---

[1] Volume I, page 56, of my edition.

trait of Shelley, that one of the rude sketches, mentioned as
being on the cover of the book, represents a pool of tranquil
water surrounded by rocks,—a good haunt wherein to write
poetry and sail fleets of paper boats.

The copy of *Queen Mab* mentioned above as having Shelley's
manuscript marks transcribed in it by Middleton was sold by
Messrs. Puttick and Simpson on the 17th of November 1880.
It was announced and catalogued as containing copious emendations in the autograph of Mrs. Shelley ; but, on my pointing out
to the auctioneers that the writing was certainly not Mrs.
Shelley's, they sold the book simply on its merits.   It is rather
to record that the current report of a copy emendated in Mrs.
Shelley's writing has no foundation than because of its own intrinsic interest that this example of the *editio princeps* is specially
described here.   It is by means of a note signed " C. S. M.", in
the same writing as the transcriptions, that Middleton's hand is
traced.   The volume was half-bound, with the margins considerably ploughed away ; but it nevertheless fetched £30.

A far more interesting copy was sold by Messrs. Sotheby,
Wilkinson and Hodge in August 1879 for £58, and was bought
by Messrs. Ellis and White, of 29 New Bond Street, who sold it to
Mr. Brayton Ives of New York.   This was the copy given by
Shelley to Mary Wollstonecraft Godwin, his future wife, and
written in by her in July 1814.   Inside the cover at the beginning
is written hastily in pencil in Shelley's hand " Mary Wollstonecraft Godwin, P. B. S." ; and inside the other cover, also hastily
written in pencil, are the words " You see Mary I have not forgotten you ".   The title-page and imprint are cut out (with a
knife, as usual) ; but the dedication to Harriett is left in, and
beneath it is written by Shelley, very carefully in ink,—

" Count Slobendorf was about to marry a woman, who
attracted solely by his fortune, proved her selfishness by desert-
ing him in prison."

I have no data for the elucidation of this reference ; but there
is likeness enough between the names *Slobendorf* and *Slabrendorf*
to justify the insertion of the following extract from Godwin's
Memoirs of the Author of a Vindication of the Rights of Woman
(1798, page 102, or in the second edition of the same year, page
105) : " Another person, whom Mary always spoke of in terms of
ardent commendation, both for the excellence of his disposition,
and the force of his genius, was a Count Slabrendorf, by birth, I
believe, a Swede."

What the younger Mary Godwin wrote at the end of the

copy of *Queen Mab* given to her by her future husband is as follows:

"July 1814. This book is sacred to me and as no other creature shall ever look into it I may write in it what I please —yet what shall I write—that I love the author beyond all powers of expression and that I am parted from him dearest & only love—by that love we have promised to each other although I may not be yours I can never be anothers. But I am thine exclusively thine

> By the kiss of love the glance none saw beside
> The smile none else might understand
> The whispered thought of hearts allied
> The pressure of the thrilling hand

I have pledged myself to thee and sacred is the gift. I remember your words—you are now Mary going to mix with many and for a moment I shall depart but in the solitude of your chamber I shall be with you—yes you are ever with me sacred vision

> But ah I feel in this was given
> A blessing never meant for me
> Thou art too like a dream from heaven
> For earthly love to merit thee."

The end-paper bearing this inscription has been refastened into the book at some time since the writing was done, and the final syllable of the word *understand* is hidden. Hence in the auctioneers' catalogue the word *under*, which is all that remains visible, was printed as *render*. I wrote to the editor of *The Athenæum* to correct this error; and my letter was mainly transferred to *The Times*, and thence to a great number of provincial and other papers, without any one of the editors and correspondents concerned remarking that the two quatrains were quotations from Byron. When at length some one pointed this out, there were actually suggestions that, this being so, the writing could not be Mrs. Shelley's! Nothing could be more nonsensical. The writing *is* Mrs. Shelley's; and the moral of the tale is that we do not care so much about Byron's songs as our parents and grandparents did; so that lines which were in every one's mouth in 1814, and were the most natural for a young girl, circumstanced as Mary Godwin was, to express herself in, are now of such small account that those who are most interested in poetry pass them unrecognized. Whether the lines were original or quoted had no bearing whatever on the genuineness of the book. I may mention that, when the volume was sold, it was in the original boards, and with the edges uncut.

A fourth copy of *Queen Mab* of special interest is mentioned in Lowndes's Bibliographer's Manual. This was a copy which had the broadside *Declaration of Rights* bound up with it; but for the present it is not forthcoming.

The copy in the British Museum has inserted in it, beside Shelley's letter of the 22nd of June 1821, cut from *The Examiner*, and his portrait cut from the frontispiece of Galignani's edition of Coleridge, Shelley and Keats, a second newspaper cutting headed

LAW INTELLIGENCE.

COURT OF CHANCERY, Aug. 26. [1817[1]]

PRIVATE HEARING.—QUEEN MAB.

WESTBROOKE *v.* SHELLEY, ESQ.

The stage of the proceedings in regard to Shelley's children reported under this heading is the appeal of the father against the choice of a guardian:

"The choice of the plaintiffs met the approbation of the Master [in chancery], who made a report to that effect, to which, however, the defendant made some exceptions. Accordingly, Messrs. Hurt, Horne, Wetherell and Montague, were this day heard on the exceptions, at considerable length.

"The LORD CHANCELLOR said, that on reading over the affidavits and documents, he would give his judgment; and this should be the case certainly before he went to the country."

At the end of the volume are two notes, both in the same handwriting, which will be presently referred to in dealing with Clark's edition. The first published edition of *Queen Mab*, as far as I have been able to ascertain, was that of Clark, mentioned in several of Shelley's letters of 1821:—

(22)

𝔔ueen 𝔐ab./ BY/ PERCY BYSSHE SHELLEY./ 𝔏ondon:/ PRINTED AND PUBLISHED BY W. CLARK,/ 201, STRAND. 1821.

This edition, an octavo, usually consists of title-page, pages 3 to 89 of text, fly-title *Notes* with note by Clark at the back, pages 93 to 182 of Notes, and a leaf bearing on the recto six advertise-

[1] Inserted in manuscript.

ments of books published by Clark. In some copies the Dedication, upon the omission of which Shelley congratulated himself, is inserted either after the title-page or at the end of the notes. Clark's remarks before the voluminous notes of the poet are as follows :

" It will be seen by the author of QUEEN MAB, and those few gentlemen who have a copy of the former edition, that I have been studious in adhering to the original copy. The notes in French, Latin, and Greek are printed verbatim, as the classical scholar would prefer them in the language they were originally written in, and the general reader in translation.

W. CLARK."

This fairly represents the facts of the case. The book is a tolerably accurate reproduction ; and translations of the notes in foreign languages are supplied as foot-notes. At page 105 *cœteris paribus* is rendered *making allowances on both sides*, which " every schoolboy " will regard as indefensible, and which does not even square with the context. Who is responsible for these translations I do not positively know ; but one of the manuscript notes mentioned above as being in the British Museum copy of Shelley's edition is as follows :

" The Greek, Latin, French, &c. Notes, translated by a Learned Linguist & Scholar a Mr. Fleming. E. H."

The imprint of Clark's edition is

" Printed and Published by W. Clark, 201, Strand.

𝕿. 𝔐."

of which " T. M." I have seen no plausible explanation, and can only suggest in default of a better that the initials indicate the printer by whom Clark got the work done,—some man wise enough in his generation to let Clark bear the brunt of his own venture, as Shelley's printer had done before. The first of the advertisements at the end of the volume is—

" Queen Mab, a Poem, in nine Cantos, with Notes and Translations. By Percy Bysshe Shelley, in one elegantly printed Vol. 8vo, uniform with the other Works of that celebrated Author. Price 12s. 6d. bds."

(23) There are copies of this edition on thick fine paper, which were probably the " elegantly printed " ones referred to : the ordinary ones are not of a high quality as to get-up. But there is a much more important variation : some copies contain the whole text and notes intact, while

others have a few of the most aggressive passages mutilated by omission of words and even verses.   These mutilations occur at pages 39, 54, 55, 65, 77, 82, 98, 146, 147-8, and 171.   The omissions at pages 146 and 147-8 are such as to involve the over-running of the pages up to 160 inclusive ; but I have not the slightest doubt about the two kinds of copy having been printed from the same types at the same period.   The other manuscript note referred to above as in the British Museum copy of Shelley's edition is as follows :

" Privately printed for Presentations.
" This is an Original Copy. Mr. Thorpe the eminent Bookseller of Piccadilly offered Ten guineas for a Copy, Twenty pounds have been given through the medium of the public papers, prior to Mr. Clark Bookseller in the Strand published it, for which he was prosecuted and tried at the Old Bailey on giving up the remainder of the copies to the Society for the Suppression of Vice he was pardoned.
" Clark only sold 50 Copies ".

How far these particulars are to be relied on I know not : Clark's edition, both mutilated and unmutilated, is very common, but whether sold by him is a more doubtful matter, as will be presently seen.   As to his trial, there is the following passage in a list of libel prosecutions in *The Republican* for the 18th of March 1825 :

" John Jones was prosecuted by the Vice Society ... The trial was called on in October 1823 ... This we understand to have been the last interference of the Vice Society : though William Clark was indicted later than Jones and brought to trial earlier for the publication of ' Queen Mab.'   Sentence four months imprisonment in Cold Bath Fields Prison."

Whether or not Clark suspended the issue of his edition, with his title-page, certain it is that some copies of the same sheets passed into the hands of Carlile, who, in the year after their publication by Clark, reissued them with the following title :—

(24)

QUEEN MAB./   by/ PERCY BYSSHE SHELLEY./ 𝔏on=
𝔡on:/ PRINTED AND PUBLISHED BY R. CARLILE,/
55, FLEET STREET./   1822.

The copy of this reissue before me has the Dedication after

the title-page and consists for the rest of the unmutilated issue
of Clark : so does the copy at the British Museum ; but that has
the Dedication at the end.   Carlile does not even seem to have
attempted to give verisimilitude to his imprint by removing that
of Clark at the foot of the last page by means of a cancel leaf ;
and he left the fly-title to the Notes undisturbed.

    With the same title and Dedication Carlile issued some
(25) copies of the unmutilated poem without the notes ; and
    in 1823 he again reissued Clark's unmutilated sheets,
with the Dedication at the end, and with the following title-
page :

(26)

QUEEN MAB ;/ A/ PHILOSOPHICAL POEM :/ WITH
    NOTES./   BY/ 𝔓𝔢𝔯𝔠𝔶 𝔅𝔶𝔰𝔰𝔥𝔢 𝔖𝔥𝔢𝔩𝔩𝔢𝔶./ [the three
    mottoes from Voltaire, Lucretius, and Archimedes given
    by Shelley in his edition] 𝔏𝔬𝔫𝔡𝔬𝔫 :/ PRINTED & PUB-
    LISHED BY R. CARLILE, 55, FLEET STREET./ 1823.

In connexion with these issues of Carlile's, I transcribe from
The Republican for the 27th of December 1822 the following
notice to which reference has already been made in connexion
with the question of the rarity of the *editio princeps* :

QUEEN MAB.

    " THERE are now no less than four editions of this work on sale,
but I would caution all my friends against an imperfect edition
selling under the imprint of William Clark.   I was not aware of
it until within the last week.   At 5, Water Lane, Fleet Street,
perfect copies may be had under my imprint at 7*s.* 6*d.* in bds.
and any other copies selling under my name are not for my
profit or under my controul.

    " I have also purchased the whole of the remaining copies
of the original edition printed by Mr. Shelley in 1813.   There
were but 180 copies left, and these will be sold at the same price
in sheets to those friends of Mr. Shelley, or others, who may
prize an original copy.   The difference in the original and my
present edition is, that the notes of the latter are all translated.
The imperfections of the copy selling under the imprint of
William Clark, consist in the exclusion of all those words and
sentences which some simpleton considered libellous.   They

E

were sold by the Printer at little better than waste paper price,
and are now put forth as perfect copies.

RICHARD CARLILE."

In the meantime had appeared what is called the first
American edition:

(27)

QUEEN MAB;/ A/ 𝔓𝔥𝔦𝔩𝔬𝔰𝔬𝔭𝔥𝔦𝔠𝔞𝔩 𝔓𝔬𝔢𝔪./ BY/ *PERCY
BYSSHE SHELLEY./* NEW YORK :/ PRINTED BY BALD-
WIN AND CO. CORNER OF/ CHATHAM STREET./ 1821.

This is a duodecimo consisting of 10 pages of unpaged preliminary matter beside the title, a blank leaf, pages 3 to 88 of text,
pages 89 to 181 of Notes, and one page of advertisements. Some
copies have an engraved title-page in addition to the printed one:
after Shelley's name this has a caduceus and the imprint " New
York,/ Printed & Sold By J. Baldwin,/ Corner of Chatham Street./
1821./ Price 75 cents." And in some copies this is the only
title-page, while others have the words *Philosophical Poem* in the
printed title in Roman letters instead of Old English. After the
title or titles comes a Preface of three pages signed " A Pantheist." The writer says he got a copy of the private edition
from Shelley in the spring of 1815, being then in England. He
adverts to the prosecution of Clark by the Society for the Suppression of Vice, says the little edition has been done for " cheapness and portability," recommends the octavo edition for libraries
as if he knew it was still to be had, and reprints Shelley's letter
to *The Examiner* out of "justice to him." After this letter comes
an " Ode to the Author of ' Queen Mab.' " This " A Pantheist "
says was written by a friend of his early in 1815: it is signed
" R. C. F." Then comes an Argument said to be from " a
Polemical Magazine published in London in 1815." At the end of
this extract the source is specified as " Theological Enquirer, by
Erasmus Perkins." The following paragraph is from the Preface :

" The object of the projectors of this edition, was cheapness
and portability, in order that it might come into the hands of
all classes of society ; consequently it was thought that translations of those passages in the notes, quoted from Greek, Latin,
and French authors, would be acceptable. This has been done
with the greatest fidelity ; and the Editor pledges himself that
there is no variation throughout this volume from the original,
except four places in the notes, where the translation is substituted for the French and Greek, with a view to render the book
less expensive."

The book is a substantial reprint, but not a perfectly accurate one. It is not easy, perhaps not possible, to decide whether it is a reprint of Clark's edition or of Shelley's; for there are details in which it varies from both; but I lean to the supposition that it was reprinted from Clark's. It may be worth noting that while " A Pantheist," when substituting translations for the Greek, Latin, and French of the notes, makes use of other translators than those used by Clark, he adopts that worthy's rendering of *cœteris paribus.* I am wholly sceptical about the *bona fides* of the imprint, and, judging from the general appearance, should think the book was printed in England, with an American imprint on account of the libel prosecutions against publishers of *Queen Mab.* The fact that American editions of later date, described further on, entirely ignore this edition, tends to confirm such a hypothesis.

A Pocket edition of less than half the size and weight of that described above was issued in 1826:

(28)

QUEEN MAB./ by/ PERCY BYSSHE SHELLEY./ 𝔏on=
𝔡on :/ PRINTED FOR THE JOINT STOCK BOOK/ COMPANY,/ AND
PUBLISHED BY RICHARD CARLILE,/ 135, FLEET STREET./ 1826.

This is a trigesimo-secundo consisting of title-page, pages 3 to 64 of text, and, in what I take to be the earliest copies, pages 65 to 132 of Notes, the imprint being *Printed by R. Carlile, Fleet Street.* These copies ending at page 132 do not give the quotation from Plutarch with which the book should end. But there are other copies in which this defect is supplied by the addition of an English version and of the Dedication, making the book end with page 135, which bears the same imprint as the other copies bear. This alteration was made by reprinting from page 129. The edition seems to reproduce Clark's; but in the notes it has the translations from Greek &c. in the place of the originals instead of appending them to the originals. Copies in the original boards have a label on the front cover, " QUEEN MAB,/ 𝔄 𝔓𝔥𝔦𝔩𝔬𝔰𝔬𝔭𝔥𝔦𝔠𝔞𝔩 𝔓𝔬𝔢𝔪,/ WITH NOTES./ *Price* 2*s.* 6*d.*" In allusion, doubtless, to this edition, one Allen Davenport, contributing to *The Republican* for the 15th of December 1826 some " Remarks on the Genius and Writings of the late Mr. Percy Bysshe Shelley," says :

" There needs no stronger proof of intellectual improvement amongst the common people than a cheap edition of ' Queen

Mab,' the price of which is reduced from half-a-guinea to half-a-crown! And I see no reason why 'The Revolt of Islam,' if it be qualified to teach every great principle, should not through the medium of the cheap press, follow 'Queen Mab' to the hands of the mechanic and labourer.

"I shall now conclude by subjoining the following lines, which were written on reading a cheap edition of 'Queen Mab' soon after the death of Mr. Shelley."

As the funny stanzas composing Mr. Davenport's "Postscript" were evidently written in sober seriousness, and help to illustrate the career of Shelley's most widely known poem, I shall be pardoned for introducing their dulness to my readers:

> Sing weeping Muse! ah, sing awhile of him,
> Who conquer'd prejudice, and broke her fetters—
> Tore from the mind the intellectual film,
> And half reform'd the dreaming world of letters.

> Wildly majestic, daringly sublime,
> Though future worlds ne'er occupied his care
> Of conscious life beyond the reach of time,
> He had no hope, and, therefore, felt no fear.

> A god superior to humanity,
> His philanthropic mind ne'er understood ;
> The cant of priests to him was vanity,
> The heaven he sought was that of doing good.

> And yet shall his imperishable mind,
> Deeply engraved on adamantine pages,
> Excite the admiration of mankind,
> Through an eternal chain of future ages.

> The philosophic *Plato* reason'd well,
> Who stamp'd the soul with immortality,
> For, though in prime of manhood SHELLEY fell,
> His *soul* still lives,—" Queen Mab " can never die!

> Could he be wrong : his " life was in the right:"
> Because in things unknown he would not trust,
> Can God spurn such a man, and, with delight,
> Smile on the pious knave ? Then God's unjust.

The year 1829, marked in the annals of Shelley literature as the year of the first revival, produced a handsome octavo edition of *Queen Mab*,—not a reissue, but a fresh reprint of Shelley's edition. It commences with an engraved title-page, its only one, which is worded as follows :

(29)

QUEEN MAB/ BY/ PERCY BYSSHE SHELLEY./ [vignette.]
Δὸς ποῦ στῶ, καὶ τὴν γῆν κινήσω./ *Archimedes./* LONDON./
JOHN BROOKS, 421, OXFORD Sᵀ./ MDCCCXXIX.

The centre is filled by a sufficiently elegant and well executed vignette drawn by C. Landseer and engraved by Portbury, representing the naked Ianthe asleep and Queen Mab summoning her spirit with outstretched wand. The title-page is followed by a single leaf bearing the Dedication ; and the volume consists, for the rest, of pages 1 to 112 of text, fly-title *Notes*, and pages 115 to 223 of Notes, ending with the imprint *London : printed by R. Brooks, Oxford Street.*

In the next year appeared

(30)

QUEEN MAB,/ or/ THE DESTINY OF MAN./ a philo-sophical poem./ by/ PERCY BYSSHE SHELLEY./ REVISED EDITION./ free from all the objectionable passages./ LONDON :/ STEPHEN HUNT, TAVISTOCK STREET./ 1830.

This is a duodecimo pamphlet consisting of fly-title *Queen Mab*, title-page as above with imprint at back, *London : Charles Wood and Son, Printers, Poppin's Court, Fleet Street*, pages v and vi of " Advertisement " signed " C. R.", and pages 1 to 62 of text ending with a repetition of the imprint given at the back of the title-page. The " objectionable passages " amount to about eight hundred lines besides the notes, so that this edition only consists of some seventeen hundred lines of verse and no notes.

Whatever may have been done in 1821, another decade at all events was not to go by without its American edition : the next to be described is

(31)

QUEEN MAB :/ with/ NOTES./ by/ PERCY BYSSHE SHELLEY./ second edition./ NEW-YORK :/ WRIGHT & OWEN./ mdcccxxxi.

This is a tall duodecimo, consisting of title-page, Dedication, " Notice of Shelley, by the American Publishers," occupying pages v to viii, pages 9 to 65 of text, and pages 67 to 120 of Notes. The publishers, who in a later American edition are mentioned as Frances Wright and R. D. Owen, " the first American publishers " of *Queen Mab*, are enthusiastic in their admiration of Shelley as a man and a reformer, commend especially the Notes to *Queen Mab*, tell our cousins the poet was the son of Sir John

Shelley, who "disinherited him on account of his opinions, or rather of his honesty in expressing them," revert to the accidental spelling *Claudiam* for *Claudiani* of Shelley's note from that author, and ascribe the extract from Plutarch to Plautus, so as to make the book end on a strictly comic note. They follow the pirates of England in substituting translations for Greek &c. in the Notes, and stick bravely to Clark's rendering of *cæteris paribus.* If, as I see no reason for doubting, the Owen of the publishing firm was, as indicated in the later American edition, Robert Dale Owen, we have here a possible ground for Medwin's statement that *Queen Mab* was the Gospel of the Owenites (see page 37). The next edition on my list has also its bearings on that point, and is a curious variation from the usual run of the piratical editions, though it too stands by Clark in the matter of *cæteris paribus* : it is

(32)

QUEEN MAB./ by/ PERCY BYSSHE SHELLEY./ London :/ PRINTED AND PUBLISHED BY MRS. CARLILE AND SONS,/ 25, BRIDE LANE, FLEET STREET./ 1832.

This is a vigesimo-quarto consisting of fly-title *Queen Mab*, title-page, pages 3 to 135 of text with Shelley's Notes distributed as foot-notes, and the Dedication to Harriett occupying page 136, which ends with the imprint *Printed by Mrs. Carlile and Sons, 25, Bride Lane, Fleet Street.* For the Greek &c. in the Notes we have translations. Probably Mrs. Carlile and her Sons counted upon the more studious of the radical mechanics of that decade, to whom *Queen Mab* was a much more serious affair than it seemed in 1821 to Shelley ; but the edition appears to have passed, in the year after its issue, into the hands of Mr. Brooks, whose Owenite customers may be presumed to have found it very convenient to have the text and notes of their Gospel arranged in the fashion here adopted. Mr. Brooks's title-page runs thus :

(33)

QUEEN MAB ;/ with/ NOTES./ by/ PERCY BYSSHE SHELLEY./ London :/ JOHN BROOKS, 421, OXFORD STREET./ MDCCCXXXIII.

This legend is repeated on the recto of a yellow wrapper, prettily printed with a line round the edge and corner ornaments suggestive of Roger Payne. The same wrapper occurs on copies with the Carlile title, so that it seems likely Brooks acquired with the stereotyped plates a certain quantity of quire stock, and used this before inserting his own title-page, which takes the place of the Carlile title and fly-title. On the verso of the wrapper are Brooks's advertisements, among which I find the following :

	s.	d.
A very handsome Edition of QUEEN MAB, with Notes, by PERCY BYSSHE SHELLY [sic], 8vo.	9	0
Ditto, in 18mo.	1	6
REVOLT of ISLAM, 8vo. By the same Author.	10	6
ROSALIND and HELEN. Same Author . .	5	6
CENCI. Same Author.	4	6
ADONAIS. Same Author . . .	2	0
SIX WEEKS' TOUR, small 8vo. Same Author	5	0
MORAL PHYSIOLOGY, 9th edition. By R. D. OWEN	1	0
OWEN'S LECTURES, each	0	3

It is to be presumed that the two editions of *Queen Mab* were that of 1829 and that now under notice, that *Rosalind and Helen* was a remainder of the original edition, *The Cenci* the second edition, *The Revolt of Islam* and *Six Weeks' Tour* the reissues of 1829, and *Adonais* the Cambridge edition of 1829. The several Shelley books were advertized in *The Athenæum* in 1832, with the exception of the smaller *Queen Mab*. This small edition passed into another publisher's hands, whether in quires, or in the form of stereotyped plates, or both, I cannot determine. There is an undated issue with a new title-page as follows :—

(34)

QUEEN MAB ;/ A PHILOSOPHICAL POEM :/ WITH NOTES./ BY/ PERCY BYSSHE SHELLEY./

" Falsehood's trade,
Shall be as hateful and unprofitable
As that of truth is now."

LONDON :/ H. Hetherington, 13, Kingsgate Street, Holborn ;/ J. Watson, 33 Windmill Street, Finsbury Square ;/ and all booksellers.

This title-page is on a different paper from the rest of the book in the only copy I have seen, and so is page 136, which ends with the imprint *Printed and Published by H. Hetherington*,

13, *Kingsgate Street, Holborn, and J. Watson, 33, Windmill Street.*
The above-named copy is extremely dirty, regularly used up
by some person or persons whose way of life did not admit of
much nicety : this points again to the radical mechanic.

Another undated edition of Watson's, issued first in 1840 or
1841, is noted in the British Museum copy as received in March
1841 : the title-page runs thus :—

(35)

QUEEN MAB :/ A PHILOSOPHICAL POEM./ 𝔚𝔦𝔱𝔥
𝔑𝔬𝔱𝔢𝔰./ BY/ PERCY BYSSHE SHELLEY./ TO WHICH
IS ADDED,/ A BRIEF MEMOIR OF THE AUTHOR./
LONDON :/ JAMES WATSON, 15, CITY ROAD ;/ NEAR
FINSBURY SQUARE.

This is a foolscap octavo. The Memoir, purporting to be a reprint of that in Galignani's 1829 edition of the Poetical Works,
immediately follows the title-page, and occupies pages 3 to 15 ; on
page 16 is the Dedication ; the text occupies pages 17 to 67, and
the Notes pages 68 to 112. At the foot of page 112 is the imprint,
Watson, Printer, 15, City Road, Finsbury. Here again translations are substituted for the Greek &c. of the Notes.   This is a
good specimen of cheap printing.   Sometimes the book occurs
in a drab paper cover, and sometimes in cloth ; and a copy
recently turned up bound in leather stamped at the side with the
words " Society for Promoting Christian Knowledge "—a grim
jest enough.   This edition appears to have been stereotyped ;
for copies obviously worked from the same type or plates occur
with various dates and addresses.   For example, in one reissue
the imprint on the title-page is " London : J. Watson, 3, Queen's
Head Passage, Paternoster Row.   1847 "—in another " London :
Published for James Watson, By Holyoake and Co., 147, Fleet
Street.   1857."   Copies of this latter date were on sale up to
1861 ; and I dare say later : I still have a copy bought in that
year to supplement Mrs. Shelley's three-volume edition of the
Poetry.   By then the plates were badly worn ; but the general
appearance of early copies, especially the undated ones, fully
justifies a statement made by Mr. W. J. Linton about Watson's
work :—

" He but asked if a book ought to be read instead of pro-
hibited, would it be useful to his class ; then he calculated how
cheaply it could be brought out, content if all his business re-
turns were sufficient for the simplest necessaries of life and to

enable him to publish more . . . You may tell a man's character
by everything he does : this man's was to be seen in a penny
pamphlet. Good matter, carefully edited, on fair paper, cleanly
printed, squarely folded, thoroughly stitched, in plain but always
neat binding or wrapper : you could not but see that it was done
by a conscientious worker, gifted with a keen sense of fitness
and propriety." [1]

His stereotyped edition of *Queen Mab* may be held to conclude the history of that work's active life on this side of the
Atlantic. The poem has played its part in the growth of free-
thought among the British working classes : henceforth it will
have its place among the juvenilia of the supreme lyrical poet.
It was probably early in the career of Watson's edition that
another tiny pocket copy came out undated—

(36)

QUEEN MAB./ BY/ PERCY BYSSHE SHELLEY/ CAMPE'S EDITION./
NURNBERG AND NEW YORK/ PRINTED AND PUBLISHED BY/ FREDE-
RICK CAMPE AND C^O.

This is a vigesimo-quarto on thin bluish paper,—text, pages
3 to 58, Notes pages 59 to 120. I have only met with it done
up in cloth together with Campe's edition of Coleridge's *Ancient
Mariner* &c.

There has been at all events one other trans-Atlantic edition
since Watson's was set up, namely

(37)

Queen Mab ;/ WITH/ NOTES./ BY PERCEY BYSSHE
SHELLEY./ FOURTH EDITION./ New-York :/ PUB-
LISHED AT "THE CITIZEN OF THE WORLD"
OFFICE,/ CHATHAM SQUARE, (No. 1 BOWERY.)/ 1852.

This is an octodecimo pamphlet with a printed wrapper almost
word for word the same as the title, even to the redundant *e* in
Shelley's first name. It is apparently a reprint of Wright
and Owen's edition : their " Notice of Shelley," described as

---

[1] JAMES WATSON/ a Memoir/ of the Days of the Fight for a Free Press/ in
England and of the Agitation for the/ People's Charter/ by/ W. J. Linton./
[motto] Manchester :/ Abel Heywood and Son, Oldham Street. [1880]—
Pages 26-8.

"by the first American Publishers (Frances Wright and R. D.
Owen)", follows the title-page, occupying pages iii to vi : the text
is on pages 7 to 66, and the Notes on pages 67 to 122, followed by
4 pages of advertisements.   This reprint is faithful to Wright
and Owen's "Claudiam" and "Plautus" and once more gives
currency to Clark's bold rendering of *cæteris paribus*.

It will be seen that Shelley's next three ventures have their
connexion with the portentous volume of his nonage ; and for the
rest, the history of the vicissitudes of *Queen Mab* will not be
exhausted for the patient reader until he shall have examined
what relates to that book under the head of COLLECTED EDITIONS.

A VINDICATION OF NATURAL DIET.

After the issue of *Queen Mab* in 1813, the note on vegetarianism beginning at page 211 of Shelley's edition was made
the substance of *A Vindication of Natural Diet*, a duodecimo
pamphlet consisting of fly-title, title-page as given below, pages
1 to 39 of text, and pages 41 to 43 of Appendix.

(38)

A

VINDICATION

OF

NATURAL   DIET.

———

BEING ONE IN A SERIES OF NOTES TO QUEEN MAB
A PHILOSOPHICAL POEM.

Ιαπετιονιδη, παντων περι μηδεα ειδωσ,
Χαιρεισ μεν πυρ κλεψασ, και εμασ φρενασ ηπεροπευσασ ;
Σοιτ᾽ αυτω μεγα πημα και ανδρασιν εσσομενοισι.
Τοισ δ᾽εγω αντι πυροσ δωσω κακον, ω κεν απαντεσ
Τερπωνται κατα θυμον, εον κακον αμφαγαπωντεσ.
                                   ΗΣΙΩΔ. Op. et Dies. 1. 54.

———

𝕷𝖔𝖓𝖉𝖔𝖓 :
PRINTED FOR J. CALLOW, MEDICAL BOOKSELLER, CROWN
COURT, PRINCES STREET, SOHO,
By SMITH and DAVY, Queen Street, Seven Dials.
1813.

———

Price One Shilling and Sixpence.

Internal evidence shows the pamphlet to have followed and not preceded *Queen Mab*. The alterations and additions are not very important; but the tract is highly characteristic. There is a copy in the British Museum with the bottom of the title-page (including the date) torn off. The fly-title is also wanting. My own copy is perfect, uncut, and in the original drab wrapper, and is the only one I ever saw or heard of beside that in the Museum and one in the possession of the Hon. J. Leicester Warren. I believe this little treatise was reprinted as an appendix to an American Medical work (Dr. Turnbull's *Manual on Health*, New York, 1835); but, not having been able to see a copy of that book, I cannot say whether the pamphlet or the *Queen Mab* note is there reprinted.

The British Museum copy has inserted in it a cutting from a newspaper evidently of the year 1822—a ribald paragraph relating to Lord Byron and to the finding of the bodies of Shelley and Williams. "One Monsieur M.," says the writer, "to all appearance the common friend of Lord Byron and of them, performed the rites of sepulture on a funeral pile, in a manner altogether antique, philosophical, and pagan—not in the least christian. The end and object of this disgusting farce must have been to collect the ashes of those two Liberals; and we shall learn, no doubt, that they are to be inclosed in two urns of Carrara marble." Alluding to a report that a certain Marquis de Voyer d'Argenson had had his dead mistress's body burnt and her ashes vitrified, causing two rings to be made set with pieces of the glass thus obtained, the obscene journalist suggests that Byron should have an emerald made of Shelley's ashes and a ruby of Williams's.

English journalism in 1822 was brutish enough for anything; but in the absence of positive information as to the source of the extract in question, there is some ground for pushing the disgrace across the Atlantic and leaving it for our relations there to adjust; for on the back of the cutting are advertisements with something much more decided than a flavour of America. Besides mention of "a good Stout Pacing Horce, lately from Tennessee," and "superior Kentucky Tobacco, for sale by Washington Jackson, No. 22 South front Street," we have an allusion to "South Third Street," and "Cheap Dry Goods"—a thoroughly American expression.

The *Vindication* has been separately reprinted by the Vegetarian Society from my edition of Shelley's Prose Works. This reprint consists of title-page, 4 pages of preface signed H. S. S.

and W. E. A. A., reproduction of original title-page, pages 9 to 27 of text, and 5 pages of advertisements. The title runs thus :—

(39)

A/ VINDICATION/ OF/ NATURAL DIET./ BY/ PERCY BYSSHE SHELLEY./ A NEW EDITION./

> " Our simple life wants little, and true taste
> Hires not the pale drudge Luxury to waste
> The scene it would adorn, and therefore still
> Nature, with all her children, haunts the hill."
> *Epipsychidion.*

LONDON : F. PITMAN, 20, PATERNOSTER ROW./ MANCHES-TER: JOHN HEYWOOD, RIDGEFIELD ; AND OFFICES/ OF THE VEGETARIAN SOCIETY, 75, PRINCESS STREET./ 1884.

This title is repeated on the verso of a grey paper wrapper, which has in addition in the right-hand upper corner the words " Price 3d." The preface may be safely attributed to two eminent members of the vegetarian sect, Mr. H. S. Salt and Mr. W. E. A. Axon. On the third page it is said of Shelley—

" We cannot doubt that if he had lived in the present time he would have taken a leading part in the movement towards Food Reform. As it is, he has left us an invaluable legacy in his ' Vindication of Natural Diet,' perhaps the most powerful and eloquent plea ever put forward in favour of the Vegetarian cause."

I have not a very wide acquaintance with the literature of Vegetarianism ; but if Shelley's poor little pamphlet is its best thing, I fear the cause is " in a parlous state."

A REFUTATION OF DEISM.

A Refutation of Deism, Shelley's next published work, is a very boldly printed octavo, consisting of title-page, pages iii to v of Preface in double pica type, a leaf with list of *errata* on recto, and 101 pages of text, with head-lines, *Eusebes and Theosophus* (the names of the interlocutors), throughout. I do not know whether this book had a printed label : the only copies I have seen are bound. The title-page runs thus—

(40)

A

REFUTATION

OF

DEISM:

IN

A DIALOGUE.

ΣΥΝΕΤΟΙΣΙΝ.

London:
PRINTED BY SCHULZE AND DEAN,
13, POLAND STREET.

1814.

Mr. Hogg, at pages 484-6 of Volume II of his Life of Shelley, gives an account of this book, which he thinks was published at *the beginning* of the year 1814. It is another offshoot from *Queen Mab*, repeating, and reconstructing in a different form, much from the Notes to that work, which Notes, however, it leaves far behind in point of literary merit. Mr. Hogg describes it as "very incorrectly printed"; but beyond the seventeen verbal errors corrected in the list, and probably arising from indistinct writing, I have only found five. In February 1843, a small extract from this work was printed in *The Model Republic* (q.v.), as from "an unpublished work" of Shelley; and in May of the same year this curious little radical monthly gave its readers a large excerpt, the passage from "Design must be proved" to "principles of reason" occupying pages 63 to 78 of the second volume of my edition of the Prose Works (1880), but with the omission of the Greek note at page 70. Thus Hogg had been forestalled in his revelation of Shelléy's authorship of the book. No copy was recovered to the public till 1874: on the 19th of June in that year a copy was bought by the Trustees of the British Museum.

Mr. Garnett possesses a second copy; and a third is in the hands of Professor Edward Dowden, who had the luck to buy it off a perambulating book-cart for twopence. Mr. Dowden thinks it is Shelley's presentation copy to Mary Shelley, as it is bound in calf with the word "Mary" stamped in gilt letters on the side. There is no inscription in it; but the *errata* of the printed list are all inserted in what Mr. Dowden believes to be Shelley's writing.

In 1875 the excerpt given in *The Model Republic* was reprinted as a separate pamphlet, with the following title-page (repeated on the wrapper with an additional line above the date,— namely, " LONDON: SIMPKIN, MARSHALL AND CO."):—

(41)

SCINTILLA SHELLEIANA./ SHELLEY'S ATTITUDE TOWARDS RELIGION,/ EXPLAINED AND DEFENDED BY HIMSELF./   EDITED BY/ ARTHUR CLIVE./

" Scatter, as from an unextinguished hearth
Ashes and sparks, my words among mankind."

DUBLIN :/ WILLIAM McGEE, 18 NASSAU STREET./
MDCCCLXXV.

This is a pamphlet of 27 pages, apparently foolscap octavo ; but, the edges being cut off, the size is uncertain. Of the 27 pages the third is a Dedication " to the youth of Ireland ", pages 5 to 9 are a sensible though somewhat utopian Preface signed " Arthur Clive "—a pseudonym of Mr. Standish O'Grady ; and pages 11 to 27 are the text, including the Greek note omitted from *The Model Republic*.   After that note the Editor says " See Goodwin's Translation of Plutarch's Essays, Tract I, Book 5."   The signature of Shelley is printed at the end as " PERCY BYSHE SHELLEY."

ALASTOR &c.

The volume containing *Alastor* and other poems is a foolscap octavo, consisting of title-page, 4 pages of preface, a fly-title *Alastor ;/ or,/ the Spirit of Solitude./* with quotation from St. Augustine, and 101 pages of text, including the respective fly-titles to the *Poems* and *The Dæmon of the World*.   At the foot of page 101 is the imprint *Printed by S. Hamilton, Weybridge, Surrey*.   This tastefully printed little volume was issued in drab boards with a printed back-label which reads " SHELLEY'S/ POEMS."   The title-page runs thus :—

(42)

ALASTOR;

OR,

THE SPIRIT OF SOLITUDE:

AND OTHER POEMS.

BY

PERCY BYSSHE SHELLEY.

LONDON:
PRINTED FOR BALDWIN, CRADOCK, AND JOY, PATER-
NOSTER ROW; AND CARPENTER AND SON,
OLD BOND-STREET:
By S. Hamilton, Weybridge, Surrey.

1816.

The poems printed in the *Alastor* volume, which has no table of contents, are (1) the Stanzas addressed to Coleridge, headed ΔΑΚΡΥΕΙ[1] ΔΙΟΙΣΩ ΠΟΤΜΟΝ ΑΠΟΤΜΟΝ, (2) Stanzas, April, 1814, (3) *Mutability*, (4) the Stanzas on the verse of Ecclesiastes, "There is no work, nor device," &c., (5) *A Summer-Evening Church-yard*, (6) Sonnet *To Wordsworth*, (7) Sonnet, *Feelings of a Republican on the Fall of Bonaparte*, (8) *Superstition* (an excerpt from *Queen Mab*), (9) Sonnet from the Italian of Dante, (10) Sonnet, Translated from the Greek of Moschus, (11) *The Dæmon of the World* [Part I]. This volume seems to have become scarce as early as 1824, for Mrs. Shelley says, in her preface to the *Posthumous Poems* of that year, "I have added a reprint of 'Alastor, or the Spirit of Solitude':—the difficulty with which a copy can be obtained is the cause of its republication." Whether this scarcity arose from the steps taken by Shelley to advertize *Alastor* along with his later works I cannot say; but he appears eventually to have put the book into the hands of Messrs. C. and J. Ollier. In an unpublished letter to Mr. C. Ollier dated the 8th of August 1817, he informs that gentleman of the issue of *Alastor* "some time since" and says that the sale was "scarcely anything," but that he has received the printer's account, and would like to have the publisher's: he remarks of the publisher "he had no interest in the work nor do I know that anyone else had." On the 3rd of December he

---

[1] A misprint (for "ΔΑΚΡΥΣΙ") which has been perpetuated almost down to the present day.

writes that *Alastor* ought to be advertized at the end of the advertisement of *Laon and Cythna*, adding that in the event of a demand for a second edition of *Alastor* he would reprint it "with many others" in his possession. Messrs. Ollier advertized the book as their own publication in *Rosalind and Helen* in 1819, and were still advertizing it in 1820 in *Prometheus Unbound.*

There is a private reprint of the book in octavo, namely

(43)

ALASTOR, OR THE SPIRIT OF SOLITUDE, &c./
Edited, with notes, by H. Buxton Forman,/ and printed for
private distribution./ MDCCCLXXVI.

This consists of leaf with Printer's certificate as to issue, title-page as above with bibliographical note at back, title-page as in original, Preface pages 7 to 9, fly-title as in original, text of *Alastor* pages 13 to 38, fly-title *Poems*, and text of poems pages 41 to 62. The issue consisted of 50 copies on ordinary paper, 25 on Whatman's hand-made paper, and 5 on vellum.

Another reprint of this volume is—

(44)

ALASTOR;/ OR,/ THE SPIRIT OF SOLITUDE:/ AND
OTHER POEMS./ BY/ PERCY BYSSHE SHELLEY./
A FACSIMILE REPRINT OF THE ORIGINAL EDITION,/ FIRST PUBLISHED
IN 1816./ LONDON : 1885 :/ REEVES AND TURNER,
196, STRAND,/ AND/ B. DOBELL, 62, QUEEN'S
CRESCENT, N.W.

The foregoing title is the first of eight preliminary pages : on the verso is a note to the effect that the issue consists of 4 copies on vellum, 50 on Whatman's hand-made paper, and 350 on "toned paper." A prefatory note by Mr. Dobell occupies pages iii to viii. For the body of the book the particulars of the *editio princeps* of course answer. There is a final leaf bearing on the recto the imprint *Reprinted at the Chiswick Press, by C. Whittingham and Co., Tooks Court, Chancery Lane.* This is a page-for-page reprint, pretty, useful, and accurate in essentials, but not a fac-simile. *The Athenæum* (8 August 1885) points out some minute variations and one misprint,—*with* for *within* at page 34, line 4 from the foot.

A PROPOSAL FOR PUTTING REFORM TO THE VOTE THROUGHOUT THE KINGDOM.

A Proposal for Putting Reform to the Vote throughout the Kingdom is an octavo pamphlet of one sheet, consisting of title-page as given below and 13 pages of text, without head-lines and numbered centrally.

(45)

𝔄 𝔓roposal

FOR PUTTING

REFORM TO THE VOTE

THROUGHOUT THE KINGDOM.

BY THE HERMIT OF MARLOW.

LONDON:
PRINTED FOR C. AND J. OLLIER,
3, WELBECK STREET, CAVENDISH SQUARE;
By C. H. Reynell, 21, Piccadilly.

1817.

Of the two pamphlets issued in 1817 under the pseudonym of "The Hermit of Marlow," this one on Reform was clearly considerably the earlier. In an extant letter to Mr. Ollier, dated the 14th of March, Shelley asks "How does the pamphlet sell?"—a question which cannot refer to the Address on the Death of the Princess Charlotte, as that event did not occur till the 6th of November. The date given in Shelley's manuscript of the pamphlet as that on which the meeting should be held at the Crown and Anchor Tavern, the 17th of March, also, of course, points to this as the pamphlet enquired after. It is fortunate that this manuscript (that used by the printer) has escaped destruction and distribution, having been kept by Mr. Ollier, and sold by his family in July 1877. It is written on eighteen leaves, small quarto, on one side only, somewhat hastily, with many changes and erasures, and has all the appearance of an original draft, revised. The title-page, in Shelley's writing, with the exception of the draft imprint, originally commenced differently, *A Proposal for a National Meeting of the . . .* The

F

manuscript was bought by Mr. Francis Harvey, bookseller, of 4 St. James's Street, by whose kind permission I collated it with the printed text, and noted in the Library Edition all variations and cancelled readings. These are not always by any means significant; but taken together they give us a glimpse of the measure of Shelley's fluency in writing such an address in the year 1817.

The manuscript contains, on the back of one leaf, one of the few extant examples of Shelley's draughtsmanship,—a kind of classical temple and some trees, executed with unwonted neatness, though with less spirit than the drawing of which a most admirable fac-simile may be seen in Volume II of Shelley's Prose Works. It is a curious coincidence that the proof-sheets of the Reform pamphlet, also decorated with drawings, have likewise survived. It will be remembered that Leigh Hunt says in his preface to *The Mask of Anarchy*—

" I have now before me his corrected proof of an anonymous pamphlet which he wrote in the year 1817, entitled ' A Proposal for Putting Reform to the Vote through the Country.' . . . The title-page of the proof is scrawled over with sketches of trees and foliage, which was a habit of his in the intervals of thinking, whenever he had pen or pencil in hand. He would indulge in it while waiting for you at an inn, or in a door-way, scratching his elms and oak-trees on the walls. He did them very spiritedly, and with what the painters call a gusto, particularly in point of grace. If he had room, he would add a cottage, and a piece of water, with a sailing boat mooring among the trees. This was his *beau ideal* of a life, the repose of which was to be earned by zeal for his species, and warranted by the common good. What else the image of a boat brings to the memory of those who have lost him, I will not say, especially as he is still with us in his writings. But it is worth observing how agreeably this habit of sketching trees and bowers evinced the gentleness of my friend's nature, the longing he had for rest, and the smallness of his personal desires."

The proof-sheet which called forth these remarks is at present in the hands of Sir Percy and Lady Shelley, to whom it was given by Hunt.

There is another document which can scarcely relate to any work but this pamphlet by " the Hermit of Marlow." Among the letters and manuscripts sold by the Ollier family figured an unpublished letter to Mr. C. Ollier indicating that the " Hermit " had some reason for anticipating a sale, unless indeed I am at fault in supposing this pamphlet to be the subject. It is a letter without date or postmark, and opens thus :

" I inclose you the Revise which may be put to press when corrected, & the sooner the better."

The fact that Hunt had the proof would indicate that a revise was sent ; and, as the letter is of about the year 1817 and cannot well refer to *Laon and Cythna*, it is scarcely to be doubted that it refers to the Reform pamphlet. It conveys instructions to advertize not sparingly, to get booksellers to take copies on their own account, mentioning specially Sherwood, Neely & Co. as likely to do so, and contains a list of persons to whom copies were to be sent " *from the Author.*" Now Sherwood, Neely & Co. were named as publishers with Olliers on the title-page of *Laon and Cythna* ; and the list, which is as follows, would be an extraordinary one for any work of Shelley's except this pamphlet, actually convening a meeting on the subject of Reform :—

Sir Francis Burdett M.P.*
Mr. Peters of Cornwall
Mr. Brougham M.P.*
Lord Grosvenor *
Lord Holland *
Lord Grey *
Mr. Cobbett *
Mr. Waithman *
Mr. Curran
Hon. Douglas Kinnaird *
Hon. Thos. Brand M.P.*
Lord Cochrane M.P.
Sir R. Heron M.P.
The Lord Mayor *
Mr. Montague Burgoyne
Major Cartwright *
Messrs. Taylor Sen. & Jun. of
    Norwich
Mr. Place, Charing Cross *
Mr. Walker of Westminster
Lord Essex *
Capt. Bennet M.P.*
The Birmingham Hampden
    Club (5 copies)

Mr. I. Thomas, St. Albans,
    Mon.
Mr. Philipps, Whitston, Mon.
Mr. Andrew Duncan, Provost
    of Arbroath
Mr. Alderman Goodbehere *
Mr. Jones Burdett *
Mr. Hallet of Berkshire (5
    copies)
The London Hampden Club
    (10 copies) *
The Editors of the Statesman *
    the Morning Chronicle * and
    the Independent Whig *
Mr. Montgomery (the Poet) of
    Sheffield
Mr. R. Oven of Lanark
Mr. Madocks M.P.
Mr. George Ensor
Mr. Bruce
Mr. Sturch (of Westminster) *
Mr. Creery M.P.
Gen¹. Sir R. Ferguson M.P.*

Those names against which I have put an asterisk have the word " sent " written opposite them in the list, not in Shelley's

handwriting.   The number sent would thus seem to have been
considerable ; and if the plan of unsparing advertisement was
also followed, it was not unnatural for Shelley to anticipate a
demand for the pamphlet.

AN ADDRESS TO THE PEOPLE ON THE DEATH OF
THE PRINCESS CHARLOTTE.

As far as I have yet been able to discover no copy of the
original Address to the People on the Death of the Princess
Charlotte is extant ; but there is a print bearing at the back of
the title the words *Reprinted for Thomas Rodd, 2, Great Newport
Street,*—evidence, by the bye, which fraudulent book-sellers
occasionally suppress with the aid of a knife, so as to offer the
tract as an " original copy."   This reprint is an octavo of two
half-sheets " stabbed " together without any wrapper : it consists of title-page as given below and pages 3 to 16 of text, in
eleven numbered paragraphs, and has at foot of the last page
the single-line imprint *Compton & Ritchie, Printers, Middle
Street, Cloth Fair, London.*   The pamphlet is printed in large
type set closely, without head-lines, and having the pages numbered centrally.

(46)

"WE PITY THE PLUMAGE, BUT FORGET
THE DYING BIRD."

AN

ADDRESS TO THE PEOPLE

ON

The Death of the Princess Charlotte.

BY

𝕿𝖍𝖊 𝕳𝖊𝖗𝖒𝖎𝖙 𝖔𝖋 𝕸𝖆𝖗𝖑𝖔𝖜.

In giving the Address from this source in my edition of
Shelley's Prose Works I said " It would be rash to assume the
reprint to be a fac-simile of the original ; but it has too much
character, almost, to be a bad representation of it."   Since that

time Professor Edward Dowden has communicated to me the following extract from a "Catalogue of Books and Manuscripts recently added to, or selected from the Stock of Thomas Rodd. 9. Great Newport Street . . . printed by Compton & Ritchie, Middle Street, Cloth Fair, 1843 " :—

SHELLEY (Percy Bysshe). Address to the People on the Death of the Princess Charlotte, 1s 6d .   .   .   .   8vo.

⁎ The author printed only twenty copies of this Address: the present is a fac-simile reprint.

Of course I do not regard this as proof that Rodd's reprint is what we should now call a fac-simile, or that the date of it was 1843 ; but it is likely enough that the work had not been long executed ; and the statement as to the number of copies of the original may very well have been based on trustworthy information.

The time at which this second Marlow pamphlet was written is ascertainable within a very few days. The Princess Charlotte died at 2.30 A.M. on the 6th of November 1817 : on the following day the executions which so roused Shelley took place. On the 12th Shelley wrote from Mablcdon Place (Hunt's residence) an unpublished letter to Mr. Ollier, enclosing what he had " written of a pamphlet on the subject of our conversation of the other evening ",—to be " sent to press without an hour's delay " ; and he promised to send the rest of the manuscript " before evening." He added " the subject tho' treated boldly is treated delicately."

This work is often spoken of as being entitled *We Pity the Plumage but Forget the Dying Bird*. That this is not the title is evident from the fact that the opening of the address is headed *An Address, &c.*; and in the setting of the title-page by which alone we know the tract, that of the reprint, there is nothing to justify the supposition that the words employed as a motto were meant for the title. Mr. Rodd himself gives it its proper title in his catalogue ; and he must have had good means of knowing the rights of the matter. Mr. MacCarthy (*Shelley's Early Life*, page 394) points out that Shelley may probably have adopted the words from the following passage in *The Reflector* (Volume I, page 17) : " It was pertinently said of the pathetic language which Mr. Burke, in his later writings, occasionally held on constitutional topics, that he pitied the plumage, but neglected the wounded and suffering bird."

HISTORY OF A SIX WEEKS' TOUR.

The *History of a Six Weeks' Tour* is a foolscap octavo volume, boldly printed, consisting of fly-title *History/ of/ a Six Weeks' Tour*, title-page as given below (having at the back the imprint *Reynell, Printer, 45, Broad-street, Golden-square*), Preface pages iii to vi, text of Journal pages 1 to 81, fly-title *Letters*, text of letters pages 85 to 172, fly-title *Lines/ Written in the Vale of Chamouni*, and the poem of that name pages 175 to 183. There are no head-lines, the pages being numbered centrally with large Arabic figures. The label, which reads up, not across, the back, is "SIX WEEKS' TOUR./ *Price 5s.*" The title-page runs thus:

(47)

HISTORY

OF

A SIX WEEKS' TOUR

THROUGH

A PART OF FRANCE,
SWITZERLAND, GERMANY, AND HOLLAND:

WITH LETTERS

DESCRIPTIVE OF

A SAIL ROUND THE LAKE OF GENEVA, AND OF
THE GLACIERS OF CHAMOUNI.

LONDON:

PUBLISHED BY T. HOOKHAM, JUN.
OLD BOND STREET;
AND C. AND J. OLLIER,
WELBECK STREET.

1817.

This little volume has a peculiar interest, not only from its biographical value, but as showing what Shelley's idea of a book of travels was in 1817. Careful readers will scarcely doubt that the journal kept by Mrs. Shelley was revised and to some small extent interpolated by the poet ; and the responsibility of publication is expressly thrown on Shelley at page xxi of Mrs. Shelley's preface to the *Essays, Letters,* &c. (2 volumes, 1840), where we read that " ' The Journal of a Six Weeks' Tour,' and ' Letters from Geneva,' were published many years ago by Shelley himself. The Journal is singular, from the circumstance that it was not written for publication, and was deemed too trivial for such by its author. Shelley caused it to be printed, and added to it his own letters, which contain some of the most beautiful descriptions ever written." I do not know positively whether this book preceded or followed the second Marlow pamphlet in issuing from the press ; but I see no reason for doubting that the pamphlet, a single sheet, was issued within a few days of the 12th of November, whereas the *Six Weeks' Tour* was entered in the Stationers' Register as being published by T. Hookham Jun. on the 10th of December 1817. When Mrs. Shelley says (Prose Works, Volume II, page 121) "It is now *nearly* three years since this Journey took place," I presume she is at the beginning of her task of transcribing her journal : then there was all the rest of the book to get ready, print, and bind ; and it may very well, in the busy year 1817, have been several months before the work came out.

(48)   This is one of the books of which Mr. Brooks seems to have obtained a remainder ; for in 1829 an issue was made, consisting of the 1817 sheets undisturbed in any particular except the cancelling of the fly-title and title and the insertion of a new title only varying from the old one after the word *Chamouni*, which is followed thus: "By PERCY B. SHELLEY./ LONDON :/ PUBLISHED BY J. BROOKS,/ 421 OXFORD STREET./ 1829." The label of the reissue reads *across* the back. Mrs. Shelley, in publishing her collection of Shelley's *Essays* &c. (referred to above), included both her own portions of it and Shelley's,—making some revisions and additions, which are noted in the Library Edition.

LAON AND CYTHNA.

[THE REVOLT OF ISLAM.]

The *editio princeps* of *Laon and Cythna* is an octavo volume, consisting of title-page, a blank leaf, preface pages v to xxii, fly-title to the Dedication, with quotation from Chapman's *Byron's Conspiracy* (Act III), Dedication pages xxv to xxxii, fly-title *Laon and Cythna* with quotation from Pindar,[1] and 270 pages of text.   I have heard of a copy containing advertisements dated October 1817, including one of *Laon and Cythna* itself.   The label reads thus: " LAON/ AND/ CYTHNA./ 10*s.* 6*d.*   Boards."   The title-page is as follows:

(49)

𝕷𝖆𝖔𝖓 𝖆𝖓𝖉 𝕮𝖞𝖙𝖍𝖓𝖆;

OR,

THE REVOLUTION

OF

THE GOLDEN CITY:

𝕬 𝖁𝖎𝖘𝖎𝖔𝖓 𝖔𝖋 𝖙𝖍𝖊 𝕹𝖎𝖓𝖊𝖙𝖊𝖊𝖓𝖙𝖍 𝕮𝖊𝖓𝖙𝖚𝖗𝖞.

IN THE STANZA OF SPENSER.

BY

PERCY B. SHELLEY.

ΔΟΣ ΠΟΥ ΣΤΩ ΚΑΙ ΚΟΣΜΟΝ ΚΙΝΗΣΩ.

ARCHIMEDES.

LONDON:

PRINTED FOR SHERWOOD, NEELY, & JONES, PATERNOSTER-ROW; AND C. AND J. OLLIER, WELBECK-STREET:

By B. M'Millan, Bow-Street, Covent-Garden.

1818.

Written in the Summer of 1817, the book was printed in the latter part of that year, the title-page being post-dated as usual; but, before it was regularly issued, it was suppressed for the purpose of altering the text in some particulars and changing the title.

The Revolt of Islam, being made up from the same sheets with a fresh title-page and 26 cancel-leaves, the same bibliographical particulars apply, except that the preface, having the final paragraph cancelled, ends on page xxi, and the fly-title with quotation from Pindar bears the words *The Revolt of Islam.*

---

[1] This fly-title is doubtless extremely scarce.   Beside my own copy I have only heard of one containing it.   It probably got lost through being a separate leaf, with a separate signature, *d,* coming in between two complete sheets,— unfortunately at that point where the Roman numerals of the preliminary matter end, so that its absence makes no obvious hiatus to be discovered by the binder.

The usual substituted title-page runs thus :—

(50)

THE

REVOLT OF ISLAM;

A POEM,

IN TWELVE CANTOS.

BY

PERCY BYSSHE SHELLEY.

LONDON:
PRINTED FOR C. AND J. OLLIER, WELBECK-STREET;
By B. M'Millan, Bow-Street, Covent-Garden.

1818.

Some few copies of *The Revolt* bear the date 1817, instead
of 1818 : probably a realistic compositor set up the new
(51) title-page, and his realism was only discovered after
the printing was begun. The label of this cancelled book
reads " REVOLT/ OF/ ISLAM./ 10*s.* 6*d.* Boards." The same
sheets were used again in 1829 with a third title-page
(52) similar to the foregoing, but with the imprint " *LON-
DON :/* PRINTED FOR JOHN BROOKS,/ 421, OXFORD-
STREET./ 1829." The labels are the same as in the original
issue of *The Revolt.* In the meantime some part of the stock of
cancel-leaves had, I presume, been lost; for copies of the 1829
issue of *The Revolt of Islam* not infrequently occur with
(53) *Laon and Cythna* text. Thus there are five varieties of
the book. There is a list of *errata* usually found in all
of them, but sometimes missing. I am not aware of any complete extant manuscript of *Laon and Cythna*; but Sir Percy
Shelley has the Preface and Dedication, written fair for the press
in Shelley's handwriting; Leigh Hunt published a fac-simile of
four lines in his *Lord Byron and some of his Contemporaries*;
Mr. W. M. Rossetti owns a larger fragment (24 lines,—formerly
in the possession of Hunt), of which a fac-simile was given in
some copies of Mr. Rossetti's two-volume edition of Shelley's
Poetry, and in the three-volume edition; and there is a still
larger fragment (52 lines) in my collection. The actual printed
copy of *Laon and Cythna* upon which Shelley worked to convert
the poem into *The Revolt of Islam* is also in my collection.

Such in outline is the bibliography of Shelley's longest work; but the whole history of the transaction whereby *Laon and Cythna* became *The Revolt of Islam* is so remarkable that it seems desirable to give fuller details of a transformation which is, as far as I am aware, without parallel in the history of literature.

The late Thomas Love Peacock's version of this affair first appeared in *Fraser's Magazine* for January 1860 (q.v.), in one of a series of papers on Shelley since reprinted in the author's collected works. According to Peacock, Shelley wrote *Laon and Cythna* " chiefly on a seat on a high prominence in Bisham Wood, where he passed whole mornings with a blank book and a pencil "; and this statement does not diverge materially from that of Mrs. Shelley, in her note on *The Revolt of Islam*, that " the poem was written in his boat, as it floated under the beech groves of Bisham, *or during wanderings in the neighbouring country.*" Peacock's account goes on thus :—

" This work when completed was printed under the title of *Laon and Cythna*. In this poem he had carried the expression of his opinions, moral, political, and theological, beyond the bounds of discretion. The terror which, in those days of persecution of the press, the perusal of the book inspired in Mr. Ollier, the publisher, induced him to solicit the alteration of many passages which he had marked. Shelley was for some time inflexible; but Mr. Ollier's refusal to publish the poem as it was, backed by the advice of all his friends, induced him to submit to the required changes. Many leaves were cancelled, and it was finally published as *The Revolt of Islam*. Of *Laon and Cythna* only three copies had gone forth. One of these had found its way to *The Quarterly Review*, and the opportunity was readily seized of pouring out on it one of the most malignant effusions of the *odium theologicum* that ever appeared even in those days, and in that periodical."

On this paragraph I have to observe (1) that altered passages of the poem are marked in pencil in Shelley's revised copy referred to above (page 73), so that I presume that to be the copy marked by Mr. Ollier; and (2) that the expression " induced to submit to the required changes " seems to me to correspond exactly with all we know of the matter. There is a slight variation of phrase in the *Shelley Memorials* (page 83), where Shelley is described as " convinced of the propriety of making certain alterations " : convinced of the need he no doubt was, for the alternative was a desperate one; but there is nothing in his subsequent history to countenance the idea that he regarded *Laon and Cythna* as in any way offensive. Indeed, when *The Quarterly Review*[1] returned after the lapse of over forty years, in a milder spirit, to the attack on Shelley, in regard to this poem, Peacock[2] added the following supplementary account of the affair :—" Mr. Ollier positively refused to publish the poem as it was, and Shelley had no hope of another publisher. He for a long time refused to alter a line : but his friends finally prevailed upon him to submit. Still he could not, or would not, sit down by himself to alter it, and the whole of the alterations were actually made in successive sittings of what I may call a literary committee. He contested the proposed alterations step by step : in the end, sometimes adopting, more frequently modifying, never originating, and always insisting that his poem was spoiled." Since this matter was debated in my edition of Shelley's poetry, many of his letters to Mr. Ollier have been sold publicly by the Ollier family. On the 25th of November 1817 the poet told his publisher to advertize at once, as the books were then ready, asking for twelve copies to be sent to him as soon as they could be "put in boards," and for one to be sent to Hunt "the first thing." In *The Examiner* for the 30th of the same month an extract from *Laon and Cythna* appeared,—one of the passages afterwards altered. On the 3rd of December 1817 Shelley wrote to Mr. Ollier in answer to some communication concerning the insertion of a list of *errata* : he described the printer as " an obstinate old dog as troublesome as he is impudent," and gave authority for him to say at the top of the list of *errata* " that it was all the author's fault, and that he is as immaculate as the Lamb of God." At the same time the poet sent Mr. Ollier advertisements for insertion in certain papers. On the 11th of December he wrote his great letter of protest against the arrest of publication (*Shelley Memorials*, pages 81-3) and on the 13th another to Mr. Ollier arranging for an immediate meeting. Then there is an undated note authorizing the publisher to get back " all the copies that have been given forth " ; and on the 27th of December 1817 Shelley wrote to Mr. Ollier expressing surprise that he had not had the remainder of the proofs (this must mean proofs of the cancel-leaves), stating that he had himself succeeded in procuring the return of "two of the copies from Ebers's," and asking whether the publisher has

---

[1] No. 220, October 1861.   [2] *Fraser's Magazine*, March 1862.

been equally fortunate in regard to " the other purchasers." " It ought to be *now*," he says, " advertised as to be published on January 10." But on January 11 he had not received copies himself, and wrote for six "instantly," following up the request on the 15th with one for ten instead of the six which had not yet been sent. On the 22nd of January 1818 Shelley wrote to Mr. Ollier—" Don't relax in the advertising—I suppose at present that it scarcely sells at all."

It is quite clear that a considerably larger number than three copies of *Laon and Cythna* " had gone forth " ; but I may as well quote some observations made in *Notes and Queries* (for April 12, 1862), by the late Mr. Denis Florence MacCarthy : he says—

" If Mr. Peacock is correct in stating that *only three copies* of *Laon and Cythna* had gone forth, the fate of these three is easily accounted for. ' One,' as Mr. Peacock says, and as is evident both from the heading and the notes of the article referred to, ' found its way to *The Quarterly Review*.' Another was certainly sent to Godwin, as we have a letter of Shelley's dated December 11th, 1817 (three weeks before the poem came out under its new title of *The Revolt of Islam*), in reply to one of Godwin's, in which he says, ' I listened with deference and self-suspicion to your censures of *Laon and Cythna*.' The third there can be no doubt was sent to Thomas Moore, ' whose most kind and encouraging letter on the subject of the poem,' Shelley had ' just received ' when writing to his publisher, Mr. Ollier, on the same day. This identical copy, with ' From the Author,' in Shelley's large bold hand-writing on the fly-leaf, is now in the Moore Library, Royal Irish Academy, Dawson Street, Dublin, where the poet's books have found an honoured resting place, owing to the liberality of Mrs. Moore. Moore's library contains also the original edition of *The Revolt of Islam*, but without any inscription from the author. I have looked carefully through both these volumes to see whether they contained any pencil marks by Moore, or any notes of admiration, condemnation, or protestation, from which we could infer whether his ' most kind and encouraging letter ' in acknowledgment was confined merely to the literary execution of the poem. I have, however, found none. It is quite plain, notwithstanding, that Shelley wished the frightened publisher to suppose that Moore might be considered in favour of the appearance of the poem in its original form.

" That Mr. Peacock's statement is strictly true is therefore extremely probable ; but that more copies were *made up* than the three that 'had gone forth' at the time of the publisher's objection to the further issue of the poem, and that these copies are now stealing into the market, is beyond all doubt.   Before alluding to the analysis which I have made of the differences existing between *Laon and Cythna*, and *The Revolt of Islam*, I may state that I have obtained two uncut copies of *Laon and Cythna* within the last six months from different London book-sellers, neither of whom, however, could assist me in my inquiries as to the way in which original copies of this poem are now getting into circulation, or as to their probable number.   That the number must be exceedingly small is, I think, evident from the parsimony almost with which the disagreeable process of cancelling the offending pages was carried out, and the eager-ness with which every printed scrap of the original sheets that was admissible was turned to use in the making up of the new volume.   An amusing instance of this may be seen in the list of 'Errata,' which is the same in both volumes.   In the process of cancelling the peccant pages, some of these errors were how-ever corrected ; but the reader of *The Revolt of Islam* is, never-theless, called upon to forgive mistakes that no longer exist (as at pages 90 and 264), except in *Laon and Cythna* ; and at page 182 line 12, the 'these' of *Laon and Cythna*, is requested to be read 'those' in the list of errata to *The Revolt of Islam*.   While in the text itself, the word 'thou,' which is different from either, is silently adopted.''

The foregoing paragraph of Mr. MacCarthy's opens up the question of the rarity of uncancelled copies of *Laon and Cythna*; and I may as well state at once that their extreme rarity is a pure fiction.   I could enumerate some dozens of copies existing within the circle of my own knowledge ; and there' are two London booksellers each of whom assures me that he some years ago bought and sold again a bundle of 25 copies done up in boards, and being, positively, the uncancelled *Laon and Cythna*.   These fifty copies (and one of the two booksellers is not sure that his bundle alone did not consist of fifty), were bought for sixpence a copy and sold in the ordinary retail way at about half-a-crown a copy ; and it is improbable that any of them have since perished ; so that they may be confidently expected to "steal into the market" some time or other.   More-over, Mr. Robert Browning, who has an unusually accurate memory for details, told me in 1876 that, when he was a youth, he met, in his wanderings about London, with a small bookseller who had for sale a large pile of copies "in quires," and that these were certainly *Laon and Cythna*, uncancelled. Of course it is possible that these copies in quires were afterwards made up into the identical two bundles in boards already mentioned; but I very much doubt this, because there was no market in those days to induce a chance owner to make up "quire stock" of any book of Shelley's; and we may better account for the two bundles in boards on the hypothesis that they were made up in 1817. The impetuous poet had probably given orders for a number to be sent out for review *immediately*; and these would be made up as soon as the book was printed. I suspect that *all* Peacock's "three copies" (very likely there were more) were sent out specially by Shelley himself;— that, before the "review copies" were despatched by the publisher, the doubts and fears so momentous to the prospects of the book arose in Mr. Ollier's mind; and that, when finally the publisher had carried his point, and had got into existence the mutilated *Revolt of Islam*, the "review copies" of *Laon and Cythna* were laid aside because it was not sure that they would be wanted at all, and it would have been more troublesome to carry out the cancelling process with them than with the "quire stock." That no such copies ever could have been wanted to supply the demand for the original edition of *The Revolt of Islam*, we know,—for "quire stock" of the uncancelled book was still in existence in 1829, when, as stated above, the book was reissued with a new title-page by a different publisher, whose copies are sometimes *Revolt of Islam*, and sometimes *Laon and Cythna* uncancelled except as regards the title-page. Within the last few years I have had in my hands a bundle of ten copies in sheets, folded, but not put up in boards, with all their labels and everything except the extremely scarce fly-title with quotation from Pindar. One of these folded copies I secured and have kept in this state among my own copies of *Laon and Cythna*; but the rest will doubtless be bound or put up in "original boards" and find their way into private collections at the usual price. These copies had remained in the family of Mr. Brooks ever since 1829.

The "parsimony" referred to by Mr. MacCarthy as characterizing the process of "cancelling the offending pages" does not, as it seems to me, affect the question of the original book's scarcity at all; and indeed I think there was rather carelessness than parsimony,—a failure to observe that a fresh list of *errata* should have been printed when some of the errors in the list had been corrected. There could be no motive of economy, for instance, in not correcting the errors specified in the list when they happened to be on a leaf that was being cancelled on other grounds; and in some instances Shelley himself, in making a change to meet Mr. Ollier's views, failed to correct on the same leaf a flagrant error which had already been detected and provided for in the list of *errata*: he would, I presume, if he thought about it, take it as a matter of course that the corrections in that list would be made without further instructions, when they happened to have reference to a leaf that was cancelled. For example, in the very case quoted by Mr. Mac-Carthy (page 77) of *thou* instead of *those* being substituted for *these*,—turning to Shelley's revised copy, I find that, when he had altered stanza viii of Canto VIII, to get rid of "God" and "his red hell's undying snakes," he made a correction in the pointing of stanza ix, *not* referred to in the list of *errata*, but did not touch stanzas x and xi, which, being on the same *leaf*, were also to be reprinted, and for which three corrections were provided in the list of *errata*. That one of those corrections was wrongly made, namely by inserting *thou* instead of *those*, I take as one indication, among others, that proofs of the cancel-leaves were sent to Shelley: I imagine that in this case, after seeing that "God" and "his red hell's undying snakes" had duly given place to "this Power" and "deepest hell and deathless snakes," he turned the leaf over and found the corrections from the list of *errata* were not made,—that he made them,—and that his *those* was, as it well might be, mistaken for *thou*. In fact, I do not see how the mistake could have occurred if the corrections had been done from the printed list; and variations in the result of his seeing proofs of the cancel-leaves would easily occur by his reading some through, and merely attending to what was altered in others. Thus he cannot have looked very closely at the cancel-leaf including stanza x of Canto XII; for, in the second line of that stanza, *waves* was reprinted, although *streams* was substituted in the list of *errata*.

Mr. MacCarthy seems to assume that the object of parsimony in such a matter would be to turn as many copies of *Laon and Cythna* as possible into copies of *The Revolt of Islam*; but in fact the object of parsimony would be to make up as few copies as possible, just enough to keep pace with the demand, and to hold the "quire stock" of the original book unmutilated in readiness for any future demand. A thousand copies of *Laon and Cythna* would have been a very moderate number for

Shelley to get printed : two hundred and fifty would have been a large number for the publisher to get cancelled and bound ; and a residue of seven hundred and fifty copies would in the natural course of things remain in quires in Mr. Ollier's warehouse, or at the printer's, with the cancel-leaves done up separately.   That some such thing *must* have happened is shown by the fact, already dwelt upon, of the original book turning up again in 1829.

One of the inconveniences of the frequent occurrence of the *Laon and Cythna* text uncancelled in the 1829 edition, called *The Revolt of Islam*, is that you have only to remove the new title-page and insert a fac-simile of the original title-page, to produce an apparently genuine copy of *Laon and Cythna*.   I have such a copy in my collection, and have seen others.

The daring idea of making radical changes in this book by means of a few cancel-leaves probably arose from the mechanical facilities which accident seems to have presented, in the mode of setting the book up ; and these same facilities have since told in favour of all sorts of bibliographical mystifications.   The book being uniformly set throughout, without foot-notes or head-lines, and with two stanzas on every page, except opening and closing pages having but one stanza each, the process of removing certain stanzas was quite simple, and the change of title only involved cancelling two leaves instead of reprinting the book, as it would have been necessary to do had the title been printed at the head of every page.   Here, the pages were simply numbered at the centre of the top, and did as well for one title as another ; and, had it not been for that fatal circumstance, it is doubtful whether there would have been any alteration whatever : probably the ease with which the book was convertible weighed with Shelley to induce him to give way ; and I cannot conceive that he would have consented to waste the whole issue of a book into which he had poured so much of his heart.   The publisher's requirements must have seemed much more formidable had they not been rounded off with the specious consideration, " all can be managed by printing twenty-eight fresh leaves " ; and but for this it seems to me Shelley would have been more likely to adopt the alternative of the withdrawal of Mr. Ollier's name from the publication,—damaging as that would have been.   It should be borne in mind that it was at Shelley's expense, and not at Mr. Ollier's, that the book was printed : it is doubtful whether Shelley at that time could have commanded funds for printing *two* such volumes one after the other; and the earnestness of his letters to Godwin and Mr. Ollier on the subject of this poem leave no room for the supposition that he would on any account have let it perish. To Godwin he says, " I felt the precariousness of my life, and I engaged in this task, resolved to leave some record of myself. Much of what the volume contains was written with the same feeling, as real, though not so prophetic, as the communications of a dying man "; and further on he speaks of the poem as having grown " as it were 'from the agony and bloody sweat' of intellectual travail."

A poem with such a genesis was not one to be readily given up by its author, or compromised by a withdrawal from publication, of which the consequences are thus described by Shelley in his letter to the publisher (*Shelley Memorials*, page 81): " You do your best to condemn my book before it is given forth, because you publish it, and then withdraw; so that no other bookseller will publish it, because one has already rejected it. You must be aware of the great injury which you prepare for me. If I had never consulted your advantage, my book would have had a fair hearing. But now it is first published, and then the publisher, as if the author had deceived him as to the contents of the work—and as if the inevitable consequence of its publication would be ignominy and punishment— and as if none should dare to touch it or look at it—retracts, at a period when nothing but the most extraordinary and unforeseen circumstances can justify his retraction."

It may perhaps be fanciful, but in the painful earnestness of Shelley's utterances concerning this poem, I seem to discern a key to the extreme corruption of the text and its striking inconsistency in minor details. The state of Shelley's mind as described by himself was such as would correspond with a very rapid and inaccurate manuscript,[1] and at the same time with a feverish desire to see the book printed accurately, which he could only, he would think, secure by revising it for the press himself. Anyone who has had much to do with printers will realize at once the result of handing over Shelley's manuscript to a printer with strict instructions to " follow copy," that is to print it *verbatim, literatim*, and point for point, and to leave the revision to the author. For those who have not had much to do with printers, let it be stated that the manuscript would in such a case (as in any other) be divided among several com-

---

[1] Indeed the manuscript fragments of *Laon and Cythna* which I have already mentioned are certainly anything but careful or consistent.

positors, that some of them would "follow copy" strictly, and that others would persistently disregard any such instruction, and correct the author wherever they thought him wrong: here I speak from positive experience, having never yet known a staff of compositors without its due proportion of men who *would not* forego their right of jurisdiction.   Then again, although in strictness the printer's reader, who goes over the whole of the proofs with the manuscript, should see that the proofs *are* "according to copy," the fact is that this is seldom scrupulously done when the instructions are, in the jocular phrase of the composing-room, "follow the copy even if it goes out of the window, and let the author revise,"—it being often improperly assumed that *he* will find out all the deviations from his manuscript.

Now the original edition of *Laon and Cythna* has to me all the appearance of a book printed under strict injunctions to "follow copy," and then revised by an author without an accurate eye for trivial detail.   Such an author we know Shelley was ; and when we come to consider the painful circumstances under which he worked at that time, we should be surprised at finding the book anything but inaccurate and inconsistent. If my hypothesis be correct, he would never discover half the mistakes of his own making which had been put into type by the compositor who "followed the copy out of the window," and which he would have wished to correct, or half the instances in which the compositor disinclined for that airy flight had altered something which *seemed* a mistake, but *was* the author's deliberate intention.

Had I known this as a fact, I could have altered, securely, much that may be found annoying in the minutely reproduced text of the Library Edition ; but as it is a mere hypothesis I could not act upon it, though I felt and still feel tolerably confident that it is the real explanation of the infamous printing of the book in question.

The revised copy of *Laon and Cythna* in my possession, spoken of above (pages 73-4) as presumably the one referred to by Peacock, is certainly the copy worked upon by Shelley to meet Mr. Ollier's views.   The foot-notes, throughout the poem, in my edition, furnish many particulars of this most interesting relic, which it was my good fortune to bring to light ; but it will be well to give here a less disjointed account of a volume which is really an important historical document, if it be true that our greatest poets are our greatest and most influential men,—or, as Shelley himself puts it, that "poets are the unacknowledged legislators of the world."

I know of few incidents in the history of literature more closely bordering on the tragic, without being actually tragical, than this dead-set made upon a great poet, who conceived that he had a gospel to preach with a view to the alleviation of the wrongs and sufferings of humanity, and who, as a dying man, desired most earnestly to leave some substantial record of what, as he deemed, it was not to be permitted him to go on delivering in person. That Shelley was not really a dying man, but only thought so by himself and certain others whose opinion ought to have been worth something, does not affect the extreme painfulness of the situation : according to the letter to Godwin already quoted, he considered himself dying, and poured his most fervent convictions into the ready mould of a poem which, if not a perfect work, was an unprecedented and truly remarkable work, full of splendour of imagination, fire of speech, purity of aspiration, and sublime disinterestedness. The question of mistaken views does not affect the matter one iota : here was this poem ready to appear before the world,—when suddenly the author was informed that it must be altered in some of its most vital particulars, or be discredited by the withdrawal of the publisher's name ; and, under extreme pressure, he altered it in those vital particulars,—wittingly but unwillingly mangled it as a work of art, and let it go forth to the world, a monument fore-doomed as it were to crumble into ruin before he whom it was designed to commemorate should be well beneath the earth. It is the good fortune of humanity that Shelley was *not* a dying man, that he lived to erect for himself a far more glorious monument than the unmutilated *Laon and Cythna*, in the noble series of works with which he followed that hapless book, given out as it were by a god maimed and shackled ; but the very series of works which he lived to leave us confers half its interest on the semi-tragic episode of the cancelling of *Laon and Cythna*, the tangible record of which episode was lost to sight for nearly sixty years, to come to light again in the fulness of that fame so tardily accorded by the poet's countrymen, but at length beyond all possibility of dispute or cavil.

My present business, however, is to give an account of the recovered evidence of his positive personal manipulation of the poem. Formerly the evidence has only been that of witnesses, —credible witnesses enough ; but there was no tangible proof of the alterations being Shelley's : now, the proof exists : the changes are certainly in his writing; while there is nothing to give a different colour to his known resistance to these changes, and clearly expressed ratification of the book as originally printed. The volume containing these changes in manuscript is, in fact, primarily, a copy of *both* the books described above, —a copy of *Laon and Cythna*, with all the cancel-leaves, printed to convert it into *The Revolt of Islam*, bound in beside the original leaves; and it contains, moreover, a single leaf of a proof-sheet of the preface to *Laon and Cythna*, showing variations of interest. The book is half-bound in a style later than that of 1818, and the edges are cut and marbled. Here and there the end of one of Shelley's letters is cut off; but, fortunately, there is no mutilation of the slightest importance to any but a bibliophile. The binder has left the sheets exactly eight inches and three-eighths in height, and here and there is a leaf with the original rough edge of the paper left,—indicating that the book was but moderately cut. The lettering on the back is "P. B. Shelley's Laon and Cythna. Cancelled Copy 1818." The words "Cancelled Copy" are also written at the head of the preface, in a large, ordinary hand,—not Shelley's, but, I incline to think, that of Mr. Buchanan M‘Millan, who printed the book.

The general appearance of the pages worked upon indicates, as would be expected, no very great respect on the part of publisher or author towards the fabric of a volume now thought so precious that it is not lawful to touch it in any but the most respectful manner; and the appearance of the binding and edges indicates that it was bound for use,—and used, though not ill used. It has had originally bound up with it, at the end, two sheets of paper very like that on which the book is printed; but the sixteen leaves of those sheets, as well as two leaves inserted between the Preface and Dedication, had been carefully removed, apparently with scissors, before the book came into my possession. What tale those leaves might have unfolded, I am at a loss to conjecture. Since the book was bound, some one has wafered in a cutting, seemingly from a provincial News-paper, containing a long review of Hogg's Life of Shelley;— and here end the external particulars.

The first point in which this copy varies from the ordinary copies is in the substituted title-page,—the *Revolt of Islam* one, —which bears the date 1817, and thus enabled me in 1876 to speak positively of a plurality of copies with that curious variation: until I got this copy I had only heard that some few of the later title-pages bore date a year earlier than the original ones ;—I knew of no specimen but that in the British Museum. Since then I have seen another cut copy, at the sale of Mr. Dew Smith's books, and have succeeded in adding to my own collection a clean uncut copy in the original boards. It is perhaps worth noting that the *Laon and Cythna* title-page of the revised copy bears no manuscript mark of any kind,—no indication of a revision of title by Shelley ; but that he did, at one point in the controversy with Mr. Ollier, furnish a second title, is proved by the fact that, on the fly-title with the quotation from Pindar, *Laon and Cythna* is erased by the poet, and *Othman* substituted by him. The finally adopted title is not in Shelley's writing, but in that of Mr. Charles Ollier : from this it might be inferred that there was a separate correspondence on the subject of title ; but as the numerous letters sold by Mr. Ollier's family in 1877 and 1878 contained no reference to title, it is perhaps more likely that that question was settled at one of the interviews of which the letters give indication.

The single leaf from the proof-sheets of the Preface to *Laon and Cythna*, which looks much as if it had been preserved as a trophy of the prowess of Mr. M'Millan, who challenged, in writing, a certain passage, has some value beyond that of showing variations. It shows that the book was undergoing scrutiny while the Preface was at press : this does not indicate, as might possibly be thought, that Shelley was under the espionage of the printer at the beginning of the printing,—for the Preface and dedication were presumably the last part *written*, and were certainly *printed* after the book, as the signatures to the sheets are " b " and " c," to distinguish them from the sheets signed " B " and " C," forming the opening of the poem ; but the inference is that the printer, who signed a manuscript suggestion to alter the words " express in the cruelty and malevolence of God " to " entertain of the Deity, as injurious to the character of his mercy and benevolence," was at the bottom of Mr. Ollier's fears about the book. I regret that there is no proof that Shelley was forced into this particular alteration, which would seem to have been adopted by him *before* the controversy with Mr. Ollier. Another point of interest in this leaf is that the fall of the lines does not correspond with the fall of the same lines in the published *Laon and Cythna* : the leaf is paged xix and xx, begins with the words " superstitious noblemen of Rome," and ends with " In recommending,"—whereas, in the book as issued, page xix has two lines before we come to " superstitious noblemen," and " In recommending " is in the third line of page xxi. From this it is to be assumed that Shelley had sufficiently worked upon the proof-sheets of the Preface, up to page xviii, to leave the printer in the necessity of carrying over two lines from that page to page xix.

Coming now to the body of the book, it is to be observed that pencilled crosses still remain against several of the altered passages, others having, it would seem, been rubbed out before the alterations were written in : there are sometimes faint indications of these crosses, and sometimes, where these should be, there is the smear apparently of a not over fresh piece of india-rubber, accompanied by the clear impression of fingers where those members would naturally be placed to hold the page steady while rubbing it.   Most of Shelley's alterations would seem to have been made by him first in pencil and afterwards in ink: most of the pencillings have been more or less hastily rubbed out; but some remain untouched beside the ink markings ; and those that remain intact are written upright, as if done constrainedly, out of doors, with no firm resting place for the wrist.   In one instance (Canto IX, stanza xiv,) where *God* was to give place to *Heaven*, that decision is noted by Shelley in pencil, merely with a capital letter *H* ; and there are other pencilled abbreviations, referred to in my notes to the poem in the Library Edition.

There are still remaining very clear traces of another kind of marking beside the crosses set against certain passages,—namely a long line drawn down beside a stanza, and a numeral put against it, not in Shelley's writing.   The numerals when traceable are consecutive, and seem to point to some written communication drawing attention to the canvassed passages *seriatim.* One of these numerical markings (" No. 7 "), for example, is at stanza xxx of Canto VI, in which, however, Shelley made no change, though he altered one word in the next stanza; and another one ignored by Shelley was " No. 10,"—at stanza xviii of Canto VII, the beautiful stanza wherein Cythna describes her baby as resembling Laon : this passage of course loses much of its significance in *The Revolt of Islam*, wherein Laon and Cythna are no longer brother and sister.

As I have mentioned above, there is nothing in this revised copy to change our views as to the preference which Shelley accorded to the original text : indeed it corresponds perfectly with Peacock's version of the affair as already quoted.

It is worth recording that Mrs. Gisborne's copy of *The Revolt of Islam,* containing many brief notes in her hand-writing, is extant and in my possession. The notes are in pencil ; and some have been rubbed out. Some of those that remain show, as we should expect, a cultivated good sense and careful reading.

ROSALIND AND HELEN &c.

Rosalind and Helen, &c., printed in the spring of 1819, is an octavo volume consisting of fly-title *Rosalind and Helen,* title-page, 2 pages of Preface (called " Advertisement "), contents, fly-title *Rosalind and Helen, a Modern Eclogue,* and text pages 3 to 92. On the back of the first fly-title are advertisements of *The Revolt of Islam* and *Alastor,* and also an imprint, *C. H. Reynell, Broad-street, Golden-square, London.* Some copies were issued in pamphlet form, with a drab wrapper, and a label reading along the back, instead of across it. I do not know whether others were issued in boards. The title-page is as follows :

(54)

ROSALIND AND HELEN,

A MODERN ECLOGUE,

WITH

OTHER POEMS:

BY

PERCY BYSSHE SHELLEY.

LONDON :
PRINTED FOR C. AND J. OLLIER,
VERE STREET, BOND STREET.
1819.

At the end of the book are four pages of Ollier's advertisements,—of works by Lamb, Hunt, Shelley, Barry Cornwall, and Ollier. The table of contents is as follows :

CONTENTS.

The Hymn had already been published in *The Examiner* for 19 January 1817, and the Sonnet (*Ozymandias*) with the signature " Glirastes " in the same paper for 11 January 1818.

In a letter to his publisher, dated " Leghorn, September 6th, 1819 " (*Shelley Memorials*, page 119), Shelley says—" In the *Rosalind and Helen*, I see there are some few errors, which are so much the worse because they are errors in the sense. If there should be any danger of a second edition, I will correct them." Whether he revised a copy, and, if so, whether Mrs. Shelley subsequently made use of it for her edition, I have no positive knowledge ; but I do not discover in the variations between her text and his any trace of such a copy, and therefore think she left these " errors in the sense " uncorrected.

In 1876, hearing that Peacock had spoken of removing Shelley's frequent dashes when revising for the press, I conjectured from the scarcity of pauses in this volume that it was to Peacock that we owed the " errors in the sense " in *Rosalind and Helen*; and some letters from Peacock to Ollier which were sold by Messrs. Puttick and Simpson on the 19th of July 1877 related to the proofs of that poem, and showed that it was he who read them.

Mrs. Shelley tells us that *Rosalind and Helen* was begun at Marlow, and thrown aside till she found it, when, at her request, Shelley finished it at the Baths of Lucca in the Summer of 1818 ; and Lady Shelley (*Memorials*, page 87) says that *a large part* of it was written in 1817 (when the Shelleys lived at Marlow) ; but it is not stated whether this was in the Spring or Winter,—before or after the composition of *Laon and Cythna*, which occupied the summer and autumn. The lapse of many eventful months may account for some of the inconsistencies in detail ; and the fact that Shelley had to be urged to finish it at all shows how little he prized it, and how little, therefore, he would have been likely to bring it up to any high degree of finish. In a letter to Peacock, written from Rome on the 6th of April 1819, while this Eclogue was being printed, the poet, after enquiring with some anxiety after the safety of his *Lines written among the Euganean Hills*, says of *Rosalind and Helen*, " I lay no stress on it one way or the other." I should imagine, therefore, that it was hastily written, and that Shelley, in the full knowledge that such was the case, deliberately declined to reduce it to perfection of detail, however willing to correct " errors in the sense." If so, to attempt to make good the omiss᠎n of rhymes and so on is extremely rash. The very imperfections have a value; and the great beauty of passages in every page becomes the more remarkable.

In giving the *Hymn to Intellectual Beauty* in *The Examiner* the Editor remarked that it was " originally announced under the signature of the *Elfin Knight.*" In the meantime the authorship had become known to the editor; and the poem was duly signed, on its appearance, with the name PERCY B. SHELLEY. I suspect that Shelley read a proof of this poem before it appeared in *The Examiner*, or else that it was pretty correctly printed from a very careful copy. The punctuation is wholly different in system from that of the version in the *Rosalind and Helen* volume; and, referring to Peacock's practice of removing the pauses so constantly used by Shelley, it should be observed that this *Hymn*, as printed in *The Examiner*, has no less than twenty-one pauses in it, while the other version has not a single one left, the whole being replaced by more orthodox points. Moreover Shelley was in England when the *Examiner* version appeared, while, from the preface to the *Rosalind* volume, it would seem that he did not even know the *Hymn* was to be in that volume,—so that he is not likely to have prepared that version. Mrs. Shelley tells us in her note on Poems of 1816 that the *Hymn* " was conceived during his voyage round the Lake [of Geneva] with Lord Byron."

As far as I am aware no entire manuscript of *Rosalind and Helen* exists; but Mr. Garnett tells me of a fragment, written in pencil in a note-book, among Sir Percy Shelley's manuscripts, —the conclusion of the poem,—presenting no variation from the printed text. Of the other three poems in the *Rosalind and Helen* volume, the only manuscripts I know of are Sir Percy Shelley's pencil draft of the *Hymn to Intellectual Beauty*, the variations shown by which belong to an early stage of the composition,—and Mr. Locker's manuscript of the interpolated passage relating to Byron in the *Lines written among the Euganean Hills*.

There is a private reprint of this volume, namely

(55)

ROSALIND AND HELEN./ Edited, with notes, by H. Buxton Forman,/ and printed for private distribution./ MDCCCLXXVI.

This is an octavo consisting of title as above with bibliographical note at back, reproduction of original title-page,

Advertisement, Contents, and second fly-title, and pages 11 to 72 of text of the four poems. The issue consisted of 50 copies on ordinary paper, 25 on Whatman's hand-made paper, and one on vellum.

THE CENCI.

The *editio princeps* of *The Cenci*, though somewhat wide in proportion to its height and approaching in shape to a quarto, is in reality an octavo, being printed on half sheets of paper folded in four. It consists of a blank leaf in place of fly-title, title-page, Dedication pages iii to v, Preface pages vii to xiv, fly-title *The Cenci* with *Dramatis Personæ* at back, and pages 3 to 104 of text, with head-lines *The Cenci* on the left hand and Act and Scene on the right. The back-label reads across, thus : " THE/ CENCI./   4s. 6d. bds." There is no printer's name on the book, the title of which runs thus :

(56)

THE CENCI.

A TRAGEDY,

IN FIVE ACTS.

By PERCY B. SHELLEY.

———

ITALY.
PRINTED FOR C. AND J. OLLIER
VERE STREET, BOND STREET.
LONDON.
1819.

Shelley told Peacock that he meant the Tragedy to be published with a frontispiece from Guido's portrait of Beatrice ; and in an unpublished letter to Miss Curran (dated the 5th of August 1819) he expressed a wish to get a good engraving done by the autumn, asking how much a " first-rate Roman artist " would demand for such a work. *The Cenci,* begun at Rome on the 14th of May 1819, was finished at Villa Valsovano, half way between Leghorn and Monte Nero, about the middle of August, and printed at Leghorn in the same year, though not published in England till the Spring of 1820, and then without the intended frontispiece. It has a few errors of the press incidental to the Italian compositors' ignorance of English, and is a characteristi-

cally irregular piece of typography ; but on the whole it seems
to me a preferable text to the second edition—a text more like
the absolute production of Shelley.   In a letter to Mr. Ollier
dated the 30th of April 1820, Shelley writes:

"I observe that an edition of The Cenci is advertised as published in Paris by Galignani.—This, though a piracy both upon
the author and the publisher, is a proof of an expectation of a
certain demand for sale that probably will soon exhaust the
small edition I sent you.[1]—In your reprint you will be guided
of course by the apparent demand.   I send a list of errata ; the
incorrectness of the forms of typography &c. which are considerably numerous, you will be so obliging as to attend to your-
self.   I cannot describe the trouble I had with the Italian
printer "—

The list of *errata*, which is in my possession, is in the hand-
writing of Mrs. Shelley.   As it has never as far as I am aware
been printed, I give it here:

"Preface. p. viii, line 2, the words *The Papal government* until
the words *a matter of some difficulty*—inclusive—to be printed as
a note.

P. xii, line 2 from the bottom, dele the word *most*.

P. 3, l. 5 from the bottom, for *so* read *as*.

P. 4, l. 9, for *respited from hell*, read, *respited me from hell*.

P. 6, last line, for *But that there*, read, *And but that there*.

P. 8, l. 6, for *have* read *had*.

P. 8, l. 15, for *shall* read *shalt*.

P. 10, l. 1, for *yet* read *thus*.

P. 11, l. 2 from the bottom, for *slave* read *vassal*.

P. 18, l. 9, for *dare not one* read *dare no one*.

P. 55, l. 2 from the bottom, read thus

> *Ors.* Why, that were well.   I must be gone ; good night!
> When next we meet may all be done ——
> *Giac.* And all
> Forgotten—Oh, that I had never been!"

Except as regards the punctuation of the last item, the whole
of these corrections were duly made in the second edition and
must be followed in future by faithful editors, unless perhaps the
alteration of the line

> But that there yet remains a deed to act

to

> And but that there yet remains a deed to act

[1] 250 copies, according to letter of 15 October 1819 (*Shelley Memorials*,
page 120).

be regarded as an imperfect fulfilment of Shelley's intention. My own impression is that he meant to cancel *yet*. But it is obvious that some of the variations concerned are true *variorum* readings and not mere errors of the press. The license given by Shelley, in the letter quoted above, in the matter of " the forms of typography," accounts for the great number of small variations between the two editions.

The Cenci is the one book of Shelley's of which a second edition appeared during his life. The London edition of 1821 is an octavo, consisting of title-page with imprint at back (*London: Printed by C. H. Reynell, Broad Street, Golden Square*), 2 pages of Dedication, Preface pages vii to xvii, fly-title *The Cenci* with *Dramatis Personæ* at back, text pages 3 to 103 with head-lines *The Cenci* in the centre, the Act being marked at the right hand of the left page and the Scene at the left hand of the right page. The imprint is repeated, with the date 1821, in the centre of page 104. The book has a back-label, reading across. The title-page runs thus :

(57)

THE CENCI

A TRAGEDY

IN FIVE ACTS

BY

PERCY BYSSHE SHELLEY

SECOND EDITION

LONDON

C AND J OLLIER VERE STREET BOND STREET

1821

Whether Mr. Reynell's reader or Mr. Ollier carried out the instruction relating to typographical irregularities, we are not informed ; but that ideal perfection was not attained I have already hinted ; and it may be well to forestall any imputation of prejudice against the second edition by pointing out that, when the Library Edition of Shelley's Poetical Works was issued, before the above quoted letter and the list of *errata* were known to exist, I recorded the suspicion that comparatively few of the minute changes in spelling and punctuation were Shelley's, and the opinion that the second edition was inferior to the first in these particulars. It is now clear that the proper basis of the text is the first edition ; and that the only legitimate revision,

beyond carrying out Shelley's corrections, is to make the detail
of the first edition text consistent in itself.

I have not succeeded in verifying Shelley's impression that an
edition of *The Cenci* was printed by Galignani; and such an
impression may have arisen from Galignani's having obtained
and advertized for sale copies of Shelley's own edition. As far
as I am aware, the third edition of this work was a piracy issued
in London, namely—

(58)

THE CENCI./ A TRAGEDY/ IN FIVE ACTS/ BY/ PERCY
    BYSSHE SHELLEY./ LONDON:/ WILLIAM BENBOW,
    252 HIGH HOLBORN./ 1827.

This is a duodecimo consisting of title-page, 2 pages of Dedication, 8 pages of Preface, fly-title *The Cenci* with *Dramatis Personæ* at back, and pages 3 to 101 of text. It has a printed
wrapper, on the face of which is the wording of the title-page
with the addition of the words " Price 2s. 6d." It is a curious
and somewhat uncommon little book, prettily but roughly
printed, from the second edition.

PROMETHEUS UNBOUND &c.

The volume containing *Prometheus Unbound*, published about
August 1820, is an octavo consisting of fly-title *Prometheus
Unbound/ &c &c* with advertisements and imprint at back, title-
page, Contents, Preface pages vii to xv, fly-title *Prometheus Unbound* with *Dramatis Personæ* at back, text of *Prometheus* pages
19 to 153 with head-lines *Prometheus Unbound*, the Act being
marked at the right hand of the left page and the Scene at the
left hand of the right page, fly-title *Miscellaneous Poems*, text of
those poems pages 157 to 222 with titular head-lines right and
left, and two pages of Ollier's advertisements ending with the
imprint (in one line) *Marchant, Printer, Ingram-Court, Fenchurch-
Street, London.* The advertisements at the back of the fly-title
are as follows:

Lately published, in 8vo. 4s. 6d.

THE CENCI: a Tragedy, in Five Acts. By PERCY BYSSHE
SHELLEY.

Also, by the same Author,

THE REVOLT OF ISLAM: a Poem, in Twelve Cantos. 8vo. 10s. 6d.

ROSALIND AND HELEN; a modern Eclogue, with other Poems. 8vo. 5s. 6d.

ALASTOR, OR THE SPIRIT OF SOLITUDE: f. c. 8vo. 5s.

Marchant, Printer, Ingram-Court, Fenchurch-Street, London.

The book is usually in drab boards; and the back-label reads " PROMETHEUS/ UNBOUND/ 9s ". The title-page is as follows:

(59)

PROMETHEUS UNBOUND
A LYRICAL DRAMA
IN FOUR ACTS
WITH OTHER POEMS
BY
PERCY BYSSHE SHELLEY
AUDISNE HÆC, AMPHIARAE, SUB TERRAM ABDITE?

LONDON
C AND J OLLIER VERE STREET BOND STREET
1820

The list of Contents is as follows:

CONTENTS.

This is almost always a cancel-leaf. I used to think that, as Mr. Ollier at one time proposed to print *Julian and Maddalo* with *Prometheus*, the original leaf might conceivably have borne the title *Julian and Maddalo* among the rest. The reason of the cancel was, however, much simpler than that. After examining a great number of copies, I found the original leaf in the one which was sold among Mr. Dew Smith's books on the 29th of January 1878; and in that copy the word *miscellaneous* had no *c* in it. Among the advertisements at the end is the following:

"HISTORY of a SIX WEEKS' TOUR through a part of France, Switzerland, Germany, and Holland; with Letters descriptive of a Sail round the Lake of Geneva, and of the Glaciers of Chamouni; foolscap 8vo. 5s."

And among "Works in the Press" is announced

"JULIAN and MADDALO, and other Poems."

There are numerous references to this, perhaps greatest volume of Shelley's works, throughout his correspondence. It would seem that a considerable portion of *Prometheus* was written in 1818. In an undated letter to Mrs. Shelley, written from Padua to her at Este, apparently in September of that year, Shelley asks her to "bring the sheets" of that poem, which she "will find numbered from one to twenty-six on the table of the pavilion"; and in a letter to Peacock dated "Este, October 8, 1818," he says, "I have been writing—and indeed have just finished the first act of a lyric and classical drama, to be called *Prometheus Unbound.*"

Mrs. Shelley records that he had meditated upon the subject, and written portions during his Italian travels between the final departure from England in the Spring of 1818 and the settlement at Rome in March 1819, but that it was only in the Spring of 1819 that he began to give it his undivided attention. Then, at all events, in the Baths of Caracalla, the first three Acts were finished before *The Cenci* was composed: he mentions *Prometheus* as "just finished"—in a letter to Peacock dated 6 April 1819, which of course refers to the three acts only; for, as Mrs. Shelley says in her note on *Prometheus*, "it was not till several months after, when at Florence, that he conceived a fourth act . . . ought to be added"; and this was not finished till near the end of December 1819. In a letter to Mr. and Mrs. Gisborne, dated "Pisa, May 26th, 1820," while accepting an offer of theirs to correct the proof-sheets, he says, "I enclose you two little papers of corrections and additions,—I do not think you will find any difficulty in interpolating them into their proper places." But on the 12th of July 1820 he writes to

Peacock, " I make bold to write to you on the news that you **are** correcting my *Prometheus*, for which I return thanks." In a letter to Mr. Ollier, dated " Pisa, November 10th, 1820," Shelley says " It is to be regretted that the errors of the press are so numerous, and in many respects so destructive of the sense . . . I shall send you the list of errata in a day or two." He does not seem to have sent it till the 20th of January 1821,—in a letter printed in the *Shelley Memorials*, but there misplaced and dated 1820 : he refers to the list as " a formidable list." Mrs. Shelley seems to have recovered it from Mr. Ollier, or to have had a duplicate, as she says in the note on *Prometheus* in her first collected edition, " the verbal alterations in this edition of Prometheus are made from a list of errata, written by Shelley himself." This must be understood with a reservation to allow for errors of the press in Mrs. Shelley's own edition. A great part of the manuscript of *Prometheus*, carefully written, is in the possession of Sir Percy Shelley : an account of some of the variations shown by it was given in *The Westminster Review* for July 1870. I presume the minor poems were printed from copies made by Mrs. Shelley ; for in an unpublished letter to Mr. C. Ollier, postmarked May 30, 1820, Shelley says " Mrs. Shelley is now transcribing for me the little poems to be printed at the end of Prometheus ; they will be sent in a Post or two." It may be worth recording that a copy of the book in my collection is inscribed on the fly-title in the hand-writing of Mr. Charles Ollier " — Coulson Esq from the Author." I presume this was " the admirable Coulson " who used to walk on Bishopsgate Heath with Shelley and Hogg.

ŒDIPUS TYRANNUS ; OR, SWELLFOOT THE TYRANT.

Œdipus Tyrannus ; or, Swellfoot the Tyrant is an octavo pamphlet of five half-sheets " stabbed " together, without a wrapper, consisting of title-page, a page of Preface called "Advertisement," with *Dramatis Personœ* at back, and text pages 5 to 39. The head-lines are, on the left-hand pages, *Œdipus Tyrannus ;* on the right-hand pages, *A Tragedy.* There is an imprint in **one** line at the back of the title-page, *Printed by C. F. Seyfang, 57, Fleet-Market.* The title-page is as follows :

(60)

ŒDIPUS TYRANNUS;

OR,

SWELLFOOT the TYRANT.

𝔄 𝔗𝔯𝔞𝔤𝔢𝔡𝔶.

IN TWO ACTS.

TRANSLATED FROM THE ORIGINAL DORIC.

———— Choose Reform or civil-war,
When thro' thy streets, instead of hare with dogs,
A CONSORT-QUEEN shall hunt a KING with hogs,
Riding on the IONIAN MINOTAUR.

LONDON:
PUBLISHED FOR THE AUTHOR,
BY J. JOHNSTON, 98, CHEAPSIDE, AND SOLD BY
ALL BOOKSELLERS.

1820.

It is a rough, common piece of printing, and has a general air of haste. The names of the speakers are usually at the beginning of the first line of each speech, abbreviated; but sometimes they are unabbreviated; and, as in *Prometheus*, they sometimes appear over the centre of the speech. I am not aware of the existence of Shelley's manuscript of this work; but a fragment of it is in the possession of Mr. H. A. Bright. In my collection is a transcript in the hand-writing of John Gisborne, stated by Miss Ramble, to whom he left it, to have been made from Shelley's manuscript; but I am disposed to think that this is a mistake, and that the transcript was really made from a copy of the pamphlet. Mrs. Shelley, reviving *Œdipus Tyrannus* in her second edition of 1839, records that it was begun in August 1820, at the Baths of San Giuliano, near Pisa; Shelley, in reading his *Ode to Liberty*, was "riotously accompanied by the grunting of a quantity of pigs brought for sale to the fair" in the square underneath the windows of his residence there; and, the struggle of George IV. to get rid of the claims of Queen Caroline being the current topic of conversation, that domestic episode seems to have combined in his mind with the porcine chorus, and to have borne fruit in this extraordinary

H

piece of intellectual grotesque, with its clear undercurrent of the same serious spirit that inspired the *Ode to Liberty* itself. "When finished," says Mrs. Shelley, "it [*Œdipus Tyrannus*] was transmitted to England, printed and published anonymously; but stiffed at the very dawn of its existence by the 'Society for the Suppression of Vice,' who threatened to prosecute it, if not immediately withdrawn. The friend who had taken the trouble of bringing it out, of course did not think it worth the annoyance and expense of a contest, and it was laid aside."

Messrs. Puttick and Simpson sold a copy of this pamphlet by auction on the 15th of May 1878; and it afterwards passed into the hands of Mr. Frederick Locker. At the top of the title-page was written, "Bought 16 Dec., 1820, M. G." The "20" has been cut off in binding, but 1820 must have been the year, to judge from the well-known facts of the case; and "M. G." would seem to have been, not Maria Gisborne, but some virtuous inhabitant of the Ward of Cheap, who bought this copy for purposes of warfare, for in the same hand-writing is written all over the title-page the following note:—

"This work was published by Johnson in Cheapside at the commencement of the Caroline Phobia; was bought by me, and presuming it to be highly libellous, some Inhabitants of the Ward determined to have it prosecuted in accordance to the resolutions of the Wardmote; it was, however, suppressed by the interference of Alderman Rothwell without coming before a Jury, the publisher giving up the whole impression, except 7 what [*sic*] he said was the whole number sold. He gave up as the Author (or at least his Employer) Smith, the Author of *Rejected Addresses, Horace in London*, &c. Smith, however, said it was sent to him from Pisa in Italy, at that time the residence of Lord Byron, Shelly [*sic*], and others."

If this is genuine (and the general air of the book, which I have examined carefully, is, or was, that of the most convincing genuineness), we learn that, whatever part the Society for the Suppression of Vice may have taken in the matter, the attack did not originate with that society; that the sale, according to Johnston, only extended to seven copies, the rest falling into hands not likely to preserve them very carefully; that Shelley's friendly agent was Horace Smith, and that that estimable gentleman staunchly refused to give up the name of his principal at Pisa; for "M. G." would certainly have said which of the "Satanic school" was the author, had he known. This copy of

"M. G." 's was, of course, one of the seven; and, if Johnston and the Ward were all good men and true, there are now only three copies to come to the surface, for this is the fourth known to Shelley specialists.   There are none in any of the public libraries, except the copy in the Dyce collection at South Kensington; the late Mr. Trelawny had a copy; and I have one. I never heard of a copy coming to the hammer before 1878 or since; and it will not be surprising if none ever comes again, for pamphlets of twenty leaves are perishable things; and even if some of the high-minded "inhabitants of the Ward" followed the example of "M. G." in preserving copies for their own reading (for "M. G." 's copy is marked in the margin throughout) still four copies would be a good percentage of survivors.

A very curious case of minute verbal and other variation is afforded by "the oracle," which first appears precisely as above on the title-page of *Swellfoot*, and then occurs twice in the text of the poem.   The oracle as uttered by PURGANAX in Act I, beginning at line 112, stands thus in the original edition:

> Bœotia, choose reform or civil war!
> When through the streets, instead of hare with dogs,
> A Consort Queen shall hunt a King with hogs,
> Riding on the Ionian Minotaur.

Here I have not the least doubt that the word *the* in the second line is a misprint for *thy*; but I do not suppose the other variations were the printer's doing; and the note of exclamation at the end of the first line seems likely enough to have been deliberate.   As repeated by the Chorus in Act II, Scene I, beginning at line 153, the oracle runs thus:

> Thebes, choose *reform* or *civil war*,
> When through your streets instead of hare with dogs,
> A CONSORT QUEEN shall hunt a KING with hogs,
> Riding upon the IONIAN MINOTAUR.

In that case a comma after *streets* in the second line seems almost necessary to the sense; and, whether Shelley or the printer dropped it, the omission must have been purely accidental.   But in regard to *your* for *thy* in the second line, and *upon* for *on* in the fourth, I should not doubt that those variations would have been left as they are, even if Shelley's attention had been called to them. If any one had asked him, "Why don't your people repeat the oracle correctly?"—he might fairly have answered, "Because real people don't repeat anything correctly in minute particulars": and, as regards the variations in the matter of italics, capitals, and so on, they probably place the stress more precisely where Shelley meant it to fall in each instance than would be the case if we ventured to print the oracle exactly alike in all three places.   This case seems to me, without being of any intrinsic importance, to afford a good example of Shelley's un-minute way of work ; and I think any textual critic who will take the trouble to compare the three versions, letter by letter, and point by point, will readily perceive how insecure must be the process of harmonizing or systematizing the text of Shelley's poems.

There is a private octavo reprint of *Œdipus Tyrannus* of (61-62) which, owing to a mistake that need not be explained, there are two varieties, neither of them having a dated special title-page, but both executed in 1876.   Both consist of fly-title *Œdipus Tyrannus ; or, Swellfoot the Tyrant*, with bibliographical note at back, title-page, Advertisement, and *Dramatis Personæ* as in the original, and pages 7 to 45 of text; but, while No. 61 has a note backing page 45, in No. 62 the same note is a fresh leaf forming pages 47 and 48 ; in No. 61 there are foot-notes to the Advertisement and *Dramatis Personæ* not given in No. 62 ; and at page 45, over the imprint of Seyfang, No. 61 has and No. 62 has not the words " The imprint of *Œdipus Tyrannus* is as follows :—".   Of No. 61, the issue was 50 on plain paper, 25 on Whatman's hand-made paper, and one on vellum,—of No. 62, 10 on plain paper, 5 on Whatman's, and 5 on vellum.

EPIPSYCHIDION.

The marvellous poetic rhapsody entitled *Epipsychidion* is a book with a reputation for being scarcer than it really is.   Rare it doubtless is ; but I have known of many copies for sale within the last ten years ; and more may be expected to come to the surface as knowledge of Shelley bibliography spreads.   *Epipsychidion* is an octavo pamphlet, sewn, without wrapper, consisting of fly-title EPIPSYCHIDION/ *Price*, 2s., title-page, 1 page of Preface called " Advertisement " with stanza from Dante at back, and text pages 7 to 31.   At the back of the fly-title is the imprint *London. Printed by S. and R. Bentley, Dorset Street, Salisbury Square*, and on the verso of page 31, in the centre, is the slightly different imprint, *London/ Printed by S & R Bentley/ Dorset Street/ MDCCCXXI.*   The title-page is as follows :—

(63)
EPIPSYCHIDION
VERSES ADDRESSED TO THE NOBLE

AND UNFORTUNATE LADY

EMILIA V——

NOW IMPRISONED IN THE CONVENT OF ——

L'anima amante si slancia fuori del creato, e si crea nel infinito un Mondo tutto per essa, diverso assai da questo oscuro e pauroso baratro.　　　　　　　　　　　　HER OWN WORDS.

LONDON

C AND J OLLIER VERE STREET BOND STREET

MDCCCXXI.

Mrs. Shelley classes the poem among those of 1821 : in a letter to Leigh Hunt dated the 29th of December 1820 (Hunt's *Correspondence*, Volume I, page 160), she seems to refer to it as already written then,—but only seems, for a part of the letter not given in the *Correspondence*, shows that there is no reference to Shelley or to *Epipsychidion* in the passage wherein those names were inserted by Thornton Hunt. Whatever the date of completion, the poem was sent to Ollier, to be published, in a letter dated the 16th of February 1821 (*Shelley Memorials*, pages 152-3), in which Shelley says, " The longer poem, I desire, should not be considered as my own . . . It is to be published simply for the esoteric few ; and I make its author a secret, to avoid the malignity of those who turn sweet food into poison ; transforming all they touch into the corruption of their own natures. My wish with respect to it is that it should be printed immediately in the simplest form, and merely one hundred copies . . . If you have any bookselling reason against publishing so small a number as a hundred, merely distribute copies among those to whom you think the poetry would afford any pleasure." I have not been able to ascertain that there is in existence any finished manuscript of the poem. Trelawny says that it was originally written in Italian.

There is a private octavo reprint of *Epipsychidion*, of (64) which, as of *Œdipus Tyrannus*, there are two varieties. Of these, No. 64 has no distinctive dated title-page (though executed the same year as No. 65, 1876), but begins with the fly-title EPIPSYCHIDION/ *Price*, 2s. with bibliographical note at back ; the original title-page is reproduced, with the stanza from Dante at back ; the " Advertisement" occupies pages 5 and 6, the text pages 7 to 26, and the studies and cancelled passages as grouped in the Library Edition pages 27 to 33. The other variety begins with the title—

(65)

EPIPSYCHIDION./ Edited, with notes, by H. Buxton Forman,/ and printed for private distribution./ MDCCCLXXVI.

This is followed by the fly-title, bibliographical note, title-page, stanza from Dante, Advertisement, and text, as in No. 64; but has not the studies and cancelled passages. The issue of No. 64 was 50 on plain paper, 25 on Whatman's hand-made paper, and 1 on vellum; the issue of No. 65, 10 on plain paper, 5 on Whatman's, and 5 on vellum.

ADONAIS.

The Pisa edition of *Adonais*, of which the title-page is reproduced below, is a small quarto, stitched, in a blue ornamented wrapper, and consists of title-page, Preface pages 3 to 5, and text pages 7 to 25,—in all three sheets and a single leaf. It has no imprint beyond that at the foot of the title-page.

(66)

ADONAIS

AN ELEGY ON THE DEATH OF JOHN KEATS,
AUTHOR OF ENDYMION, HYPERION ETC.

BY

PERCY. B. SHELLEY

Ἀστήρ πρὶν μὲν ἔλαμπες ἐνι ζώοισιν ἐῶος.
Νῦν δε θανὼν, λάμπεις ἕσπερος ἐν φθίμενοις.
PLATO.

PISA
WITH THE TYPES OF DIDOT
MDCCCXXI.

According to a letter from Shelley to Mr. Gisborne, dated the 5th of June 1821, he had been " engaged these last days in com-

posing " *Adonais*; and on the 16th of the same month he wrote
to Mr. Gisborne that it was then finished, and was sent to "the
press at Pisa " on that day: in writing again on the 13th of
July, he advised Mr. Gisborne of the despatch of the only copy
the printer had delivered.   This was a long time for the printing of a thin pamphlet, and seems to indicate some trouble given
to the printer in the shape of corrections while at press.

In 1877 I expressed the opinion that there were hardly
any printer's errors in Shelley's edition, and that the appearance of the work as well as the passages in Shelley's letters
relating to it justified the belief that here at all events Shelley
took great care in writing and revising, and was not frustrated
by the printer.   At the same time I considered that he must
have made a few manuscript changes after publication.   Among
the letters of Shelley subsequently sold by the Ollier family
was one bearing on this subject.   It is an undated letter purporting to accompany a sketch for a frontispiece to *Adonais*,
which Shelley wished to be put into the engraver's hands at once,
so that the illustration might be ready for insertion in the Pisa
book, already on its way to London.   The poet describes the
book as " beautifully printed, and what is of more consequence,
correctly."   I have also since obtained a letter of Mrs. Shelley's
in which it is stated that Shelley had wished certain alterations
made in *Adonais*.   This letter is on the subject of Galignani's
edition (q,v,), in which the most important of the changes subsequently introduced into Mrs. Shelley's own text of this poem
duly appeared.   I am not aware of any extant manuscript of
Adonais approaching completeness, or of any manuscript at all
except the passages in the note-books in Sir Percy Shelley's
possession, examined by Mr. Garnett, and said by him to be
"the merest fragments."   But even a finished manuscript would
not affect the question of the few important changes made by
Mrs. Shelley, for which I suppose she had the authority of a
copy revised by Shelley after publication.

A curious typographical detail in the Pisa *Adonais* is that
the frequent dashes, which seem to have exactly the value usual
with Shelley, are all double the usual length, except in two instances.   The fact is that, in Shelley's bold writing, these dashes
were very long: the English printers would understand this;
but Didot's people seem to have followed them literally ; and,
the book being boldly printed, this peculiarity would not be
likely to strike Shelley in revising.   The two instances in which
the ordinary dash occurs in the Pisa edition are line 5 of stanza

ix, and line 9 of stanza xxxiv. In all other cases the dashes are what printers call 2-em metal-rules.

Shelley's " intention to subjoin to the London edition of this poem a criticism upon the claims of its lamented object to be classed among the writers of the highest genius who have adorned our age " does not appear to have left any traces among his manuscripts. With the exception of stanzas xix to xxiv the poem was reprinted in a review, purporting to give the whole, in *The Literary Chronicle* for 1 December 1821 ; but I am not aware that any separate London edition of *Adonais* was ever published. The earliest separate reprint known to me is an octavo pamphlet published in 1829 at Cambridge:

(67)

ADONAIS./ 𝔄n 𝔈legy/ on the/ DEATH OF JOHN KEATS,/ author of endymion, hyperion, etc./ by/ PERCY B. SHELLEY./ [motto as in original] 𝔠ambridge:/ printed by w. metcalfe,/ and sold by messrs. gee & bridges, market-hill./ mdcccxxix.

It consists of title-page, note on a second leaf, Preface pages **v** to viii, and text pages 1 to 28. The note is as follows : " The present edition is an exact reprint (a few typographical errors only being corrected,) of the first edition of the ' Adonais,'— dated, ' Pisa, with the types of Didot, MDCCCXXI. ' " The minute variations from the original are far more considerable than the projectors seem to have been aware ; but, in essential matters, it is an accurate edition. The late Lord Houghton told me that, when at Cambridge, he and Arthur Hallam (who brought a copy of the Pisa edition from Italy), and one or two others, resolved to get it reprinted ; and, after some difficulty in finding a publisher, this was done. Lord Houghton could not recollect whether he or Hallam edited the text : but he remembered that Deighton, a proposed publisher, objected to the words " which was like Cain's or Christ's " (stanza xxxiv), and wanted to put asterisks for those names !

There is a private octavo reprint of *Adonais* (undated, (68) but executed in 1877), which consists of fly-title *Adonais* with bibliographical note at the back, title-page as in the original, Preface pages 5 to 8, and text pages 9 to 20. The issue of this reprint was 50 copies on plain paper, 25 on Whatman's hand-made paper, and 6 on vellum.

HELLAS.

Hellas, the last work which Shelley published, is an octavo pamphlet, with drab wrapper, consisting of fly-title *Hellas* with imprint at back (*Printed by S. and R. Bentley, Dorset Street, London.*), title-page as given below, Dedication, Preface pages vii to xi, fly-title *Hellas* with *Dramatis Personæ* at back, and text pages 3 to 60. The poem itself ends at page 53 of the pamphlet, where the imprint is repeated; and the Notes form pages 55 to 58 : these, again, are followed by the poem *Written on hearing the News of the Death of Napoleon*, forming pages 59 and 60. There is a label on the first side of the wrapper, reading "HELLAS/ A/ LYRICAL DRAMA/ 3s 6d". The title-page is as follows :—

(69)

HELLAS

A LYRICAL DRAMA

BY

PERCY B. SHELLEY

ΜΑΝΤΙΣ ΕΙΜ' ΕΣΘΛΩΝ 'ΑΓΩΝΩΝ
ŒDIP. COLON.

LONDON

CHARLES AND JAMES OLLIER VERE STREET
BOND STREET
MDCCCXXII

In a letter to Mr. Gisborne, dated "Pisa, October 22, 1821," printed in the second volume of Shelley's *Essays &c.* (1840), pages 332-5, we read, "I am just finishing a dramatic poem, called Hellas, upon the contest now raging in Greece—a sort of imitation of the Persæ of Æschylus, full of lyrical poetry." In a letter to Mr. Ollier dated the 11th of November 1821 (*Shelley Memorials*, page 160) he says, " I send you the drama of *Hellas*" to be sent instantly to the printer, adding " *The Ode to Napoleon* to print at the end "; and on the 11th of January 1822 he wrote to his publisher complaining that he had received no proofs of the work. A letter to Mr. Gisborne, dated "Pisa, April 10, 1822," standing next in the volume, opens thus: " I have received Hellas, which is prettily printed, and with fewer mistakes than any poem I ever published.   Am I to thank you for the revision of the press? or who acted as midwife to this last of my orphans, introducing it to oblivion, and me to my accustomed failure? . . . It was written without much care, and in one of those few moments of enthusiasm which now seldom visit me, and which make me pay dear for their visits."   A day later he requested his publisher to send his general account to Mr. Gisborne, enclosed a list of *errata* for *Hellas*, and said it was "in general more correct" than his other books.   In a letter to "C. T. Esq." (Horace Smith), he calls *Hellas* "a sort of lyrical, dramatic, nondescript piece of business."   Shelley's remark as to the comparative freedom from mistakes of course refers to essential mistakes only, and must be taken as a protection against any freedom of emendation, beyond what is authorized by the list of *errata* (see Library Edition, Volume IV, page 572); but from a technical point of view mistakes abound, as the utmost irregularity of production prevails.   For instance, the names of speakers for the first 113 lines are printed in uniform small capitals, while throughout the remainder of the drama they are in large and small capitals: then we have sometimes "Semichorus 2d,"—at others "Semichorus 2nd."   There are various other small inconsistencies, probably attributable to the printer, or to Shelley's substitute in revision.   I am not aware that any autograph manuscript of *Hellas*, beyond the fragments of the draft in Sir Percy Shelley's note-books, is now in existence; but the printer's copy, written fair by Edward Williams and revised by Shelley, is in the possession of Mr. F. Locker.   It was preserved by Mr. Ollier and sold by his family in July 1877.

    There is a private reprint of this volume, consisting of (70) fly-title *Hellas* with bibliographical note on verso, title-page and Dedication as in the original, pages 7 to 10 Shelley's Preface, fly-title *Hellas* with *Dramatis Personæ* on verso, pages 13 to 59 of text, 60 to 64 of Shelley's Notes, and the poem on Napoleon's death occupying pages 65-6.   Of this edition there were 50 copies on ordinary paper, 25 on Whatman's hand-made paper, and 5 on vellum.

POETICAL PIECES.

In 1823 "remainders" of *Prometheus Unbound* &c., *Hellas*, the second edition of *The Cenci*, and *Rosalind and Helen* &c., were made up into one volume with a fly-title *Poetical Pieces*, and the title-page

(71)

POETICAL PIECES,

BY THE LATE

PERCY BYSSHE SHELLEY;

CONTAINING

PROMETHEUS UNMASKED, A LYRICAL DRAMA;
WITH OTHER POEMS.
HELLAS; A LYRICAL DRAMA.
THE CENCI; A TRAGEDY, IN FIVE ACTS.
ROSALIND AND HELEN; WITH OTHER POEMS.

LONDON:
PRINTED FOR C. AND J. OLLIER:
AND W. SIMPKIN AND R. MARSHALL,
STATIONERS HALL COURT.
1823.

The volume consists of the original editions of these works, with their fly-titles, titles, and tables of contents. They were done up in boards uniformly with the *Posthumous Poems*, and were labelled at the back " POETICAL PIECES/ BY THE LATE/ P. B. SHELLEY./   10*s*. 6*d*.   *Boards*."

In the same year there was an issue without *Hellas*.
(72) The title was worded precisely as above except that the line relating to *Hellas* was omitted, and that the pointing of the imprint was slightly different; but the printing of the fly-title and title for this second reissue was not executed from the types that were used for the first.   This is worth noting, because the egregious blunder of printing *Unmasked* for *Unbound* thus appears to have been made twice over.   I suspect copies of both these reissues have been of tolerably frequent occurrence these last few years; but they will not be found frequently hereafter, because the booksellers have systematically slaughtered the special title-pages and rebound the component volumes.   I have a copy of the first issue containing the book-

plates (two) of Henry T. Worley, his signature dated 1826, and
the following sonnet, entitled in virtue of its ante-1829 date to
a place here:

> Shelley! high master of the mind exempt
>   From fear and foster'd prejudice—so long
>   That have enslav'd the mightiest sons of song
> Fettering each spirit dubiously that dreamt
>   That human Orizons might mount alone
>   From the pure heart to the Eternal throne
>   Marr'd by no Mediator and by Thee
>   Sole-swaying Infinite! accepted be
>   That in the fire-girt Centre—ever One—
>   Sittest with no assessor—God—nor Son—
> Blest wert thou in thy bosom's glorious Friend—
> Blest in thine early undecaying end—
> Blest in thy Genius—but more blest than all
> That no gross impious lies could thy bright soul enthrall.
> H. T. W.

POSTHUMOUS POEMS.

The series of posthumous volumes completing the first issues
of Shelley's works commences with his widow's initial in-
gathering from the disordered papers which he left.   The title-
page is

(73)

POSTHUMOUS POEMS

OF

PERCY BYSSHE SHELLEY.

In nobil sangue vita umile e queta,
Ed in alto intelletto un puro core;
Frutto senile in sul giovenil fiore,
E in aspetto pensoso anima lieta.
PETRARCA.

LONDON, 1824:
PRINTED FOR JOHN AND HENRY L. HUNT,
TAVISTOCK STREET, COVENT GARDEN.

This is an octavo volume, usually in drab boards, labelled
" POSTHUMOUS/ POEMS/ OF/ PERCY BYSSHE SHEL-
LEY./   *Price* 15*s. boards.*"   It is beautifully printed on ribbed
paper and has on the verso of the title-page the imprint
London : printed by C. H. Reynell, Broad Street, Golden Square.
There is no fly-title: the Preface occupies pages iii to viii, and

is dated "London, June 1st, 1824." The list of contents occupies pages ix to xi. Page xii is blank. The poems occupy
415 pages including the fly-titles to *Julian and Maddalo, The
Witch of Atlas,* the *Letter to* ———— [Mrs. Gisborne], *The
Triumph of Life, Fragments from an Unfinished Drama, Prince
Athanase,* the *Ode to Naples,* the reprints of *Marianne's Dream*
and *Mont Blanc,* and the fly-titles to the separate divisions of
Miscellaneous Poems, Fragments, Alastor (reprinted), and *Translations.* At the end of the volume Reynell's imprint is repeated
at the foot of an otherwise blank page.

In some copies an additional leaf is inserted after the blank
page xii, bearing a list of *errata* (26 lines) on the recto, and on
the verso the following :—

A List of MR. SHELLEY'S PREVIOUS WORKS, *which may
be had of the Publishers of the "Posthumous Poems."*

ADONAIS, 4to. sewed, 3*s.* 6*d.*
CENCI, 8vo. boards, 4*s.* 6*d.*
EPIPSYCHIDION, 8vo. sewed, 2*s.*
HELLAS, 8vo. sewed, 3*s.* 6*d.*
PROMETHEUS UNBOUND, 8vo. boards, 9*s.*
PROPOSALS FOR REFORM, 8vo. sewed, 1*s.* 6*d.*
ROSALIND AND HELEN, 8vo. 5*s.* 6*d.*
REVOLT OF ISLAM, 8vo. boards, 10*s.* 6*d.*
SIX WEEKS' TOUR, foolscap, boards, 5*s.*

This leaf has no signature; and the list of *errata* was probably
compiled after the book had begun to be circulated : hence its
frequent absence from copies.

The following letter from Mrs. Shelley to Mr. Charles Ollier
may have had reference to the scheme of the Posthumous Poems,
or merely to the plan of transferring the above-named works to
John Hunt's establishment :—

My dear Sir
     Will you have the kindness to deliver into Mr. John
Hunt's hands such copies of Mr. Shelley's works as you still
retain.—I should be very glad of a single copy of Alastor if by
any chance there should be one remaining
    I hope that Mrs. Ollier and yourself are in good health.
Your obedient Servant
Mary W. Shelley
Spelhurst Street
Octr. 28th

If the words "copies of Mr. Shelley's works" mean, as is most likely, the books published by Messrs. Ollier on commission for Shelley, it is to be assumed that the list published by John Hunt represents the stock, that the remainder of *Alastor* had been sold or given away, and that there were no copies of the *Address on the Death of the Princess Charlotte.* If the reference is to manuscripts of unpublished works, they were of course wanted for the *Posthumous Poems*; and it was probably for the same collection that Mrs. Shelley was seeking a copy of *Alastor*, which she reprinted in that volume, mentioning the difficulty with which a copy could be obtained.

That the books were again offered for sale separately after being made up twice, with different general title-pages, in the *Poetical Pieces* of the previous year, is puzzling. Why there should have been copies of that collection without *Hellas* in 1823, though Hunt was able to offer *Hellas* for sale in 1824, I do not understand. But it would seem, at all events, that the last attempt of the Olliers to sell Shelley's works was not very successful.

The table of contents of the volume of *Posthumous Poems* is as follows :

CONTENTS.

Julian and Maddalo . . . .
The Witch of Atlas . . . .
Letter to —— [Mrs. Gisborne] . . . .
The Triumph of Life . . . .
Fragments from an Unfinished Drama . . . . .
Prince Athanase . . . .
Ode to Naples . . . .
Marianne's Dream . . . .
Mont Blanc . . . .

MISCELLANEOUS POEMS.

On the Medusa of Leonardo da Vinci . . . . . .
Song [Rarely, rarely, comest thou] . . . . . .
To Constantia, singing . . . .
The Fugitives . . . .
A Lament [Swifter far than summer's flight] . . . .
The Pine Forest . . . .
To Night . . . .
Evening . . . .
Arethusa . . . .
The Question . . . .
Lines to an Indian Air . . . .
Stanzas [written in dejection near Naples] . . . .
Autumn, a Dirge . . . .
Hymn of Apollo . . . .
Hymn of Pan . . . .
The Boat on the Serchio . . . .
The Zucca . . . .

Translation from Moschus [Pan and Echo] . . . . . .
Scenes from the " Magico Prodigioso " of Calderon . . . .
Scenes from the " Faust " of Goëthe [*sic*] . . . . . .

In 1834 Ascham issued, under the title of *Posthumous Poems by Percy Bysshe Shelley*, an excerpt from his pirated edition of Shelley's Poetry. It is not properly a separate reprint of the genuine edition of Mrs. Shelley, but merely the sheets from the pirated book done up separately; and it contains, beside the Posthumous Poems, *The Sensitive Plant*. It is therefore more properly to be included under the head of the book of which it is a part. See COLLECTED EDITIONS.

THE MASQUE OF ANARCHY.

The Masque of Anarchy is a foolscap octavo volume, consisting of fly-title *The Masque of Anarchy*, title-page as under, pages v to xxx of Preface by Leigh Hunt, pages 1 to 47 of text with imprint at foot of page 47 (*London: Bradbury and Evans, Printers, Bouverie Street.*), and two pages of Moxon's advertisements. It occurs in boards of various colours, labelled along the back " SHELLEY'S MASQUE." The title-page runs thus :

(74)

THE

MASQUE OF ANARCHY.

𝔄 𝔓𝔬𝔢𝔪.

BY PERCY BYSSHE SHELLEY.

NOW FIRST PUBLISHED, WITH A PREFACE
BY LEIGH HUNT.

Hope is strong;
Justice and Truth their winged child have found.
REVOLT OF ISLAM.
LONDON:
EDWARD MOXON, 64, NEW BOND STREET.

1832.

The poem was written in 1819 on the occasion of the infamous " Peterloo " affair, and was sent to Leigh Hunt, for publication in *The Examiner*, before November 1819. Hunt did not publish

it then, but saved it till 1832, and then issued it with a preface
of considerable interest, reprinted in the appendix to the third
volume of the Library Edition. The manuscript from which the
poem was given in that edition is that sent to Leigh Hunt; and
it is headed, in Shelley's writing, *The Mask of Anarchy written
on the occasion of the Massacre at Manchester.* It is mainly in
Mrs. Shelley's hand-writing; and I am strongly under the impression that it was dictated by Shelley from his rough notes;
—for there are lines filled in in his writing, as if he had, in the
ardour of recomposition, told his amanuensis not to wait when
there was any hitch, but to go on and leave blanks for him to
fill. The insertions and corrections in his writing are made
with a much broader pen (or heavier pressure) than was used
by Mrs. Shelley; and this fact is valuable in proving that he
went over the whole manuscript very carefully after her. The
corrections in punctuation and minor detail, with the heavier
pen, are very numerous. Mr. G. I. F. Tupper produced an
excellent fac-simile of some of the altered stanzas, which will be
found in the Library Edition.

In Leigh Hunt's proof-sheets of this book (penes me) there
is abundant evidence, if such were wanted, of the earnest interest he took in his friend's work. On the title-page, the
motto from *Laon and Cythna* is inserted in Hunt's writing as an
afterthought. The Preface is the merest sketch of what ultimately appeared: there are but seven pages instead of twenty-
five; these are full of corrections; and there is a "rider" containing all the best part of the Preface, which lovers of Shelley
will ever hold dear for its admirable reply to the charge that the
poet was "an aristocrat by disposition":

"It was finely said one day in my hearing by Mr. Hazlitt,
when asked why he could not temporize a little now and then,
or make a compromise with an untruth, that it was 'not worth
his while.' It was not worth Shelley's while to be an aristocrat.
His spirit was large enough to take ten aristocracies into the
hollow of his hand, and look at them as I have seen him look at
insects from a tree, certainly with no thought either of supe-
riority or the reverse, but with a curious interest."

Against the second couplet of stanza lviii—

> "All who think those things untrue
> Of which priests make such ado"—

Hunt wrote on the proof—"If Mr. Moxon wishes these two
lines omitted, their place can be supplied by asterisks." Mr.

I

Moxon did not avail himself of this permission. The note explaining why stanzas lxxxi to lxxxiii are in italics is an afterthought, being written in the margin of the proof.

The only other independent edition of the Poem known to me bears the following title :

(75)

THE/ MASQUE OF ANARCHY./ TO WHICH IS ADDED,/ QUEEN LIBERTY ;/ SONG—TO THE MEN OF ENGLAND/ BY PERCY BYSSHE SHELLEY./ WITH A PREFACE/ BY LEIGH HUNT./

Hope is strong ;
Justice and Truth their winged child have found.
REVOLT OF ISLAM.

LONDON :/ J. WATSON, 15, CITY ROAD, FINSBURY./ 1842.

This foolscap octavo pamphlet of a sheet and a half consists of title-page, Preface pages 3 to 10, *The Masque* pages 11 to 22,—pages 23 and 24 being occupied by Shelley's version of the National Anthem and the Song to the Men of England. There is an imprint at the foot of page 24, *J. Watson, Printer, 15, City Road, Finsbury.* The pamphlet has a drab wrapper : page 1 of this repeats the title-page, with the addition of the words *Price Threepence* and a long list of booksellers. The other three pages are filled with Watson's advertisements. Mr. W. J. Linton tells me this publication was suggested by him, and that Hunt's permission was got.

THE SHELLEY PAPERS.

Our next substantive instalment of Shelley's remains is *The Shelley Papers*, republished from *The Athenæum*. This contribution of Thomas Medwin's to Shelley literature is an elegantly printed pocket volume folded in eight, but somewhat smaller than foolscap octavo. It is what booksellers not infrequently call by the somewhat questionable name "eighteenmo." The book occurs in boards of various colours, labelled at the back " SHELL.\[Y/ PAPERS./ 3s. 6d." The title-page runs thus :

(76)

𝕿𝖍𝖊 𝕾𝖍𝖊𝖑𝖑𝖊𝖞 𝕻𝖆𝖕𝖊𝖗𝖘

MEMOIR

OF

PERCY BYSSHE SHELLEY

BY T. MEDWIN, ESQ.

AND

ORIGINAL POEMS AND PAPERS

BY PERCY BYSSHE SHELLEY.

NOW FIRST COLLECTED.

LONDON:

WHITTAKER, TREACHER, & CO.

1833.

The title-page is immediately followed by the "Advertisement," and that by "LINES/ *Written by the Author of ' The Bride's Tragedy,'*[1] *in the/ blank-leaf of the ' Prometheus Unbound' *"; a table of contents occupies pages vii and viii, the Memoir pages 1 to 106 : this is followed by a fly-title *Poems and Papers/ by/ Percy Bysshe Shelley* ; the Poems occupy pages 109 to 126, the Papers pages 127 to 180. Page 180 ends with the imprint (in one line), *London : J. Holmes, Took's Court, Chancery Lane* ; and this is followed by three pages of advertisements.

---

[1] These lines by Thomas Lovell Beddoes originally appeared in *The Athenæum*, and are as follows :—

> WRITE it in gold—a Spirit of the sun,
> An Intellect ablaze with heavenly thoughts,
> A Soul with all the dews of pathos shining,
> Odorous with love, and sweet to silent woe
> With the dark glories of concentrate song,
> Was sphered in mortal earth.   Angelic sounds,
> Alive with panting thoughts, sunned the dim world ;
> The bright creations of a human heart
> Wrought magic in the bosoms of mankind :
> A flooding summer burst on Poetry,
> Of which the crowning sun, the night of beauty,
> The dancing showers, the birds, whose anthems wild,
> Note after note, unbind the enchanted leaves
> Of breaking buds, eve, and the flow of dawn,
> Were centred and condensed in his one name
> As in a providence—and that was SHELLEY.

The table of contents is as follows; but instead of the pages I give references to *The Athenæum.*

ESSAYS, LETTERS FROM ABROAD, TRANSLATIONS, AND FRAGMENTS.

Mrs. Shelley's two collected editions of 1839, though mainly reprints, added much to what we before had of Shelley's, especially the second edition. They however fall to be described in the list of collected editions, while the *Essays, Letters* &c. take their place here among the substantive first editions, notwithstanding their containing reprinted matter, as the *Posthumous Poems* had done before. The book is in two volumes, crown octavo, with titles as follows :

[1] See **Part II**, under the head of *Examiner.*

(77)

ESSAYS,

LETTERS FROM ABROAD,

TRANSLATIONS AND FRAGMENTS,

BY

PERCY BYSSHE SHELLEY.

EDITED

BY MRS. SHELLEY.

" The POET, it is true, is the son of his time; but pity for him if he is its pupil, or even its favourite! Let some beneficent deity snatch him when a suckling from the breast of his mother, and nurse him with the milk of a better time; that he may ripen to his full stature beneath a distant Grecian sky. And having grown to manhood, let him return, a foreign shape, into his century; not however to delight it by his presence, but dreadful, like the son of Agamemnon, to purify it."— SCHILLER.

IN TWO VOLUMES.

VOL. I. [II.]

LONDON:

EDWARD MOXON, DOVER STREET.

MDCCCXL.

The fly-titles read *Essays,/ Letters from Abroad,/ &c. &c.* After the title (which has at the back a central imprint, *London: Bradbury and Evans, Printers, Whitefriars*), Volume I consists of pages v to xxviii of Preface by Mrs. Shelley, dated " Putney, December, 1839," an unpaged leaf with motto from Carlyle (" That thou, O my Brother," &c.), pages xxxi and xxxii of Contents, fly-title as at the beginning, and pages 1 to 319 of text. The imprint is repeated in the centre of page 320. The title of Volume II has the same imprint as that of Volume I at the back, but differently arranged. For the rest, the volume consists of pages v to viii of Contents, fly-title *History of a Six Weeks' Tour* [&c. as in title-page of Shelley's edition], pages 3 to 46 of Preface and Journal (reprinted with slight alterations), fly-title *Letters/ descriptive of/ a Sail round the Lake of Geneva,/ and of the/ Glaciers of Chamouni*, pages 49 to 95 of those letters (reprinted), pages 96 to 106 of the posthumous Journal with Ghost stories, fly-title *Letters from Italy*, and pages 109 to 360 of those letters. At the foot of page 360 the imprint is repeated. The Contents of the volumes are—

[1] The whole fragment was named by Shelley " A Discourse on the Manners
of the Ancients, relative to the subject of Love."
* Eight letters to Hunt, marked with asterisks, had already appeared in
Hunt's *Lord Byron and Some of his Contemporaries.*

Essays, Letters from Abroad, Translations &c. 119

LETTERS FROM ITALY (*continued*).

A letter to Joseph Severn was interpolated, in subsequent editions, between LX and LXI.

The result of analysing and comparing the contents of these volumes and the contents of *The Shelley Papers* is that Medwin is left sole authority for four compositions in prose—

> Remarks on ' Mandeville ' and Mr. Godwin,
> On ' Frankenstein,'
> On the Revival of Literature, and
> A System of Government by Juries.

The poems in *The Shelley Papers* were all reprinted by Mrs. Shelley ; but the stanzas *To the Queen of my Heart*, she rejected in her second edition of 1839.

The issue of the two volumes of prose would seem to have taken place very shortly after the date of the Preface ; for on the 19th of December 1839 Mrs. Shelley wrote to Mr. Moxon on the subject of reviews which had already appeared. " The Examiner," she says, " was *really* good—*very*—the Athenæum creditable.—*But* the Spectator !—its editor must be both a goose and a coxcomb—the notion that L[ord] B[yron] had any hand in the Peter Bell is half-witted—the incapacity of appreciating the Defence of Poetry betrays a degree of ignorance rarely to be parallelled in the whole circle of criticism—to so foolish and uneducated a person the Fragments of Metaphysics must indeed appear devoid of meaning—he does not know his a. b. c. of the language in which they are written."

I presume this handsome edition of the *Essays and Letters* was not a very brisk financial success ; for up to 1844 advertisements of it still appeared in Moxon's publications. In the following year a new edition was issued ; and I have not found any advertisements of the original edition after the issue of the new one, the title of which runs thus :

(78)

ESSAYS,/ LETTERS FROM ABROAD,/ TRANSLATIONS AND FRAGMENTS./ BY PERCY BYSSHE SHELLEY./ EDITED BY MRS. SHELLEY./ [motto as in 1st ed.]/ A NEW EDITION./ LONDON :/ EDWARD MOXON, DOVER STREET./ 1845.

This is a royal octavo consisting of fly-title as in the first edition, but with the motto from Carlyle on the verso, title-page with imprint on verso, *London : Bradbury and Evans, Printers, Whitefriars*, Preface pages v to xii, Contents pages xiii to xvi, and 164 pages of text without any divisional fly-titles. Bradbury's imprint is repeated in one line at the foot of page 164.

The Preface and Contents are set in single column, the rest of the book being in two columns. The pages throughout are surrounded with double rules. The book was issued in a primrose-coloured wrapper with the title repeated on the recto. It contained, in addition to what had been previously published, a letter from Shelley to Joseph Severn, inserted as No. LXI, with a note to the effect that the original was in the possession of the Rev. T. Wilkinson. It appears to have been Mrs. Shelley's wish to add other letters; for I have a letter from her to Mr. Charles Ollier, asking whether he had any from her husband which he could let her have to publish, and adding " You will see that I have published such as I have been able to collect." This letter is undated, but must have been written between 1839 and 1845. Mr. Ollier has inscribed at the head of it " I did *not* accede to this request, because no money was offered me, and I felt the letters were valuable to me."

The royal octavo edition was stereotyped; and I believe the plates are still in existence. It has been through many vicissitudes. In 1847 it was combined with the royal octavo edition of the poetry in a single volume, and it is in that form that it is still issued. (See under the head of COLLECTED EDITIONS.) After being incorporated in the single volume it was still on sale separately; and I presume it hung on hand; for in 1850 copies of the book were in the hands of Messrs. Tegg and Co., who removed the title-pages, and made them up with other similarly printed volumes in a single royal octavo book entitled

(79)

STANDARD LIBRARY./ COMPRISING/ THE INDICA-
TOR AND THE COMPANION, BY LEIGH HUNT./
THE POETICAL WORKS OF CHARLES LAMB./
TALES FROM SHAKESPEARE, BY CHARLES
LAMB./ THE POEMS OF WILLIAM SHAKE-
SPEARE./ ESSAYS, LETTERS FROM ABROAD,
&c. BY P. B. SHELLEY./ LONDON:/ WILLIAM
TEGG AND CO., 85, QUEEN-STREET,/ CHEAP-
SIDE./ MDCCCL.

I can find no difference but the want of title-page between this issue of the prose volume of Shelley and the issue of 1845, —even the paper seems to be the same. The only other separate edition of the *Essays* &c. known to me is that in two foolscap octavo volumes, of which also I only know one issue—

(80)

ESSAYS,/ LETTERS FROM ABROAD,/ TRANSLATIONS
AND FRAGMENTS./ BY PERCY BYSSHE SHEL-
LEY./ EDITED BY MRS. SHELLEY./ IN TWO
VOLUMES./ VOL. I. [VOL. II.]/ A NEW EDITION./
LONDON:/ EDWARD MOXON, DOVER STREET./
1852.

Volume I consists of fly-title *Essays, Letters from abroad,/
Translations and Fragments*, with motto from Schiller on the
verso, title-page with imprint on the verso, *London : Bradbury
and Evans, Printers, Whitefriars*, Preface pages v to xxii, Contents pages xxiii and xxiv, fly-title *Essays, Translations, and/
Fragments*, with motto from Carlyle on the verso, and pages 3
to 259 of text, with Bradbury's imprint at foot of last page.
Volume II consists of fly-title with motto on verso as in Volume
I, title-page, Contents pages v to viii, fly-title *History of a Six
Weeks' Tour* [&c. as in title-page of Shelley's edition], pages 3
to 84 of that work and the journal with ghost-stories and on
return to England, fly-title *Letters from Italy*, pages 87 to 293 of
those letters (the imprint being repeated at the foot of page
293), and one leaf with advertisements of the royal octavo
edition of Poetry and Essays &c., and of Mrs. Shelley's three-
volume edition of the poetry. This charming pocket edition of
the *Essays, Letters* &c. was in print for many years, and was at
last done up in a single volume, but without any other change ;
so that copies of the foolscap octavo edition, two volumes in
one, are not in any sense of a separate issue.

RELICS OF SHELLEY.

Dr. Garnett's admirable contribution to Shelley literature
is a foolscap octavo volume consisting of fly-title *Relics of
Shelley*, title-page with imprint at back (*London : Bradbury and
Evans, Printers, Whitefriars*), pages vii to xiv of Preface dated
" March, 1862," pages xv and xvi of Contents, fly-title *Poems,/
Etc.*, pages 3 to 91 of " Relics " in verse and prose (anno-
tated), pages 92 to 99 "On the Text of Shelley's Poems,"
fly-title *Letters to Leigh Hunt*, pages 103 to 144 of letters from
Shelley and his wife to the Hunts (annotated), fly-title *Shelley,*

Harriet Shelley and/ Mr. T. L. Peacock/ (with motto [1]), pages
147 to 174 of Mr. Garnett's remarks on that subject, fly-title
Lines at Boscombe, pages 177 to 182 of the charming poem so
called (addressed by Mr. Garnett to the adopted child of Sir
Percy and Lady Shelley, now Mrs. Scarlett), fly-title *Appendix,*
pages 185 to 191 of Appendix containing an additional letter of
Shelley to Leigh Hunt with postscript by Mrs. Shelley, and two
pages of advertisements. At the end of page 191 the imprint is repeated. The first page of advertisements is headed
"Shelleyana published by Messrs. Moxon & Co." These are
three in number, the *Shelley Memorials,* Trelawny's *Recollections,*
and Hogg's *Life* (Volumes I and II),—a fact which should
suffice to remove the baseless heresy of the second-hand booksellers that Hogg's volumes were withdrawn. The title-page
and Contents of the *Relics* are as follows :

(81)

RELICS OF SHELLEY.

EDITED BY

RICHARD GARNETT.

"Sing again, with your dear voice revealing
A tone
Of some world far from ours,
Where music and moonlight and feeling
Are one."

LONDON:
EDWARD MOXON & CO., DOVER STREET.
1862.

CONTENTS.

[1] . "Words
That make a man feel strong in speaking truth.
TENNYSON."

THE DÆMON OF THE WORLD.

The two parts of *The Dœmon of the World* show in completeness how much Shelley in 1815 thought worth preserving of *Queen Mab*, how he revised and reconstructed those portions, and how much new work he added to the old ; and my private issue of this poem seems to come more appropriately apart than under the head of *Queen Mab* : so much, indeed, is special to the revised poem that I think the separate impression of it may properly be included in the present division of *The Shelley Library.* For an account of the copy of *Queen Mab* upon which Shelley worked to produce the fresh poem, see pages 36 to 44. The title-page of this little square decimo-sexto volume is worded thus :—

(82)

THE DÆMON OF THE WORLD

BY

PERCY BYSSHE SHELLEY

𝕮𝖍𝖊 𝕱𝖎𝖗𝖘𝖙 𝕻𝖆𝖗𝖙
AS PUBLISHED IN 1816 WITH ALASTOR

𝕮𝖍𝖊 𝕾𝖊𝖈𝖔𝖓𝖉 𝕻𝖆𝖗𝖙
DECIPHERED AND NOW FIRST PRINTED FROM HIS OWN MANUSCRIPT
REVISION AND INTERPOLATIONS IN THE NEWLY DISCOVERED
COPY OF QUEEN MAB

LONDON
PRIVATELY PRINTED BY H BUXTON FORMAN
38 MARLBOROUGH HILL
1876

The book consists of a leaf with note on verso as to the number issued (50), fly-title *The Dœmon of the World*, title, Inscription to the Memory of Thomas Wade, fly-title *Preface*, pages xi to xiv of Preface, fly-title *First Part*, Part I of the poem pages 3 to 18, fly-title *Second Part*, and Part II of the poem pages 21 to 38.

The fifty copies were all printed on the same paper,—a fine hand-made " wove " paper, the whitest I could get ; but, to avoid bibliographical puzzles in the future, it is well to record that two copies were pulled on an ugly yellow Dutch hand-made paper, which I rejected. They were not destroyed, but are stowed away somewhere, and may perhaps be found among my papers some day.

NOTES ON SCULPTURES &c.

This private print consists mainly of the unpublished Notes and Fragments which I was fortunate enough to recover while preparing the Library Edition of Shelley's Prose Works.   The short title of the book is *Notes on Sculptures*. It is an octavo consisting of fly-title, *Shelley's Notes on Sculptures &c.*, with certificate as to issue at back, title-page, Preface pages v to viii, fly-title *Notes on Sculptures in Rome/ and Florence*, pages 11 to 45 of those Notes, fly-title *The Elysian Fields,/ a Lucianic Fragment*, pages 49 to 51 of that Fragment, fly-title *On Peacock's " Rhododaphne,"* and pages 55 to 61 of the Essay on *Rhododaphne*.   At the foot of page 61 is the imprint *Printed by Ballantyne and Hanson London and Edinburgh* (it was printed in London).

The Notes which Shelley jotted down when visiting the galleries of Rome and Florence have the same spontaneity and vividness of impression that we find in the best of his inimitable letters to Mrs. Shelley, Peacock, and other favoured correspondents.   The Notes composing the series given in the private volume are sixty in number.   Of these, though only eight were given in the *Essays, Letters* &c., eleven had appeared in print before I edited them.   The eight which figure in the *Essays* had been previously printed in *The Shelley Papers* : the remaining three of those which had seen the light before they were given in my little volume had appeared in Medwin's Life of Shelley. The manuscript from which *The Elysian Fields* was given is remarkable for the pen-and-ink drawing by Shelley on the outside,—the drawing of which a fac-simile is mentioned further back (page 66). The title-page of the *Notes on Sculptures* runs thus:

(83)

NOTES ON SCULPTURES IN ROME AND FLORENCE TOGETHER WITH A LUCIANIC FRAGMENT AND A CRITICISM ON PEACOCK'S POEM "RHODODAPHNE" BY PERCY BYSSHE SHELLEY EDITED BY HARRY BUXTON FORMAN.

LONDON PRINTED FOR PRIVATE DISTRIBUTION MDCCCLXXIX

In the following year the contents of the book were published in the Library Edition. The separate issue of the *Notes on Sculptures* was limited to twenty-five copies on Whatman's hand-made paper and fifty on ordinary paper. I should mention that one or two phrases which were omitted from the Notes as published are to be found in the privately-printed volume.

THE SHELLEY LIBRARY.

I.

HIS OWN BOOKS, PAMPHLETS, AND BROADSIDES;
POSTHUMOUS SEPARATE ISSUES; AND
POSTHUMOUS BOOKS WHOLLY
OR MAINLY BY
SHELLEY.